KINGDOM
VALUES

KINGDOM VALUES

CHARACTER OVER CHAOS

TONY EVANS

BETHANYHOUSE
a division of Baker Publishing Group
Minneapolis, Minnesota

Published by Bethany House Publishers
11400 Hampshire Avenue South
Minneapolis, Minnesota 55438
www.bethanyhouse.com

Bethany House Publishers is a division of
Baker Publishing Group, Grand Rapids, Michigan

Printed in the United States of America

ISBN 978-0-7642-3882-6 (cloth)
ISBN 978-0-7642-3883-3 (paperback)
ISBN 978-1-4934-3592-0 (ebook)

Cover design by LOOK Design Studio

Baker Publishing Group publications use paper produced from sustainable forestry practices and post-consumer waste whenever possible.

22 23 24 25 26 27 28   7 6 5 4 3 2 1

CONTENTS

PART ONE

THE FOUNDATION OF BIBLICAL CHARACTER

1

WHAT IS TRUTH?

I can't breathe.

It's a statement we have all heard over the past few years. It appears on shirts, signs, hats, and in a number of other places. I'm sure you know its origins as it relates to the wrongful death of George Floyd at the knee of a policeman. But since that time, the statement has taken on a life of its own. It symbolizes a need for justice. It speaks to equality. It resounds with the hope of reforming broken systems in a broken world. It also reminds us of the stranglehold injustice can have on anyone who comes within its grip.

This statement has impacted us not only nationally, but globally. It has become personal to many of us as we have heard it said by loved ones or friends in an entirely different context: Since the onset of the COVID-19 pandemic, millions have lost their lives because of an inability to breathe. Many people have experienced the powerlessness of not being able to help their loved one breathe. Gasping for air and being placed on oxygen or on a ventilator have become all-too-familiar occurrences—whether experienced firsthand or through another's retelling of the horrors of this virus that ravages the lungs.

Yet, despite the difficulties and death all around us, you and I are living in a day when we have gathered to collectively watch yet another potential demise. Huddled in a small room barely big enough for all of us to sit or stand in, we stare as truth appears to draw its final breaths. We watch as, with each gasping inhale and struggling exhale, truth's strength diminishes before our very eyes.

Truth, which used to be a solid pillar in many people's lives, lies there on a makeshift hospital bed, a mere skeleton of its former self. Hollowed jaws and protruding bones remind us of where vibrant life used to be. We watch, waiting. Wondering if truth will somehow pull through.

After all, our culture has already proclaimed that truth is dead. Our culture has already ripped off the life support and walked out of the room. Our culture has washed its hands and said good-bye to that which used to guard our land. Our culture has effectively sought to remove the remaining safeguard preventing us from falling into an abyss of chaos and confusion.

Not only would the actual death of truth usher in greater calamity, but the process of truth's dying over the last decades has already led to a breakdown in the cultural immune system of our entire world. The starvation that has taken place in the organs and lifeblood of humanity is immense. Without truth flowing freely through the arteries of civilization, as oxygen flows through the arteries of a body, the organs that sustain order are shutting down. They are collapsing and can no longer provide what our society needs to function in a productive and healthy way.

Not much remains of honor, honesty, or character in our culture as we watch the ongoing plans for truth to not only be buried but also funeralized before us. Somewhere along the line, we have forgotten that truth matters. We have forgotten that we depend on truth far more than we realize. We have forgotten that objective standards govern much of what we choose to do; they don't govern just our values. Without truth, the whole world would collapse. Even the opponents of truth depend on it to function every day.

For example, how would you feel about flying on an airplane with an unsure pilot? If you heard your pilot come on the speaker before the flight and say, "We are about to take off, and I'm pretty sure I know what buttons to push to operate the plane properly, but sometimes I just like to mix it up," what would you do? If you are like me, you would get off that plane.

Or how would you feel about a surgeon who has discarded truth in his or her field? Let's say you were having a consultation with a surgeon and he or she said, "I watched a surgery like this the other day online and that surgeon was doing some pretty cool new things that I'd like to try to save time. I think I know just where to cut." Would you even stay for the rest of the consultation, or would you, like me, get up and walk away?

What about a pharmacist who admits to guessing about the accuracy of the dosage as your medication is put in the bottle? Would you take it? Or what if the pharmacist said, "I have a lot of meds to choose from on these shelves. Never mind what the doctor prescribed—let me pick one that I feel is right for you!"

THE FALLACY OF FEELINGS

Not long ago, I watched the Cowboys play the Eagles on Monday Night Football. One of the scoring plays Dak Prescott attempted involved his running a quarterback sneak into the end zone. It was not evident by watching it in real time whether he made it in. So the referees did what they've been trained to do. They went to the sidelines to review the film.

After they showed the play from various camera angles, it quickly became evident to all of us watching that there really was no definitive angle that showed whether he got into the end zone. Usually that means the referees will stick with the initial call—in this case, that he did not get into the end zone. But something struck me as I watched the game. One of the announcers for ESPN who is known for his experience in football said that it "felt" like Dak got in. He kept emphasizing that it just "felt" as though he scored, based on seeing the lunges of the players and the pack.

It seemed like an odd thing for an announcer to say, especially since this announcer was the one dedicated to speaking about contested referee decisions. That's when the other commentator asked him if a referee is supposed to overturn a call because of how he feels. The announcer who had emphasized feeling laughed and admitted that no, the referee should not. A call is to be overturned only when there is clear, undisputed visual confirmation that it should be overturned.

Too much of our culture today is operating on the same basis the announcer did in wanting that call overturned. Decisions are being made based on feelings. Truth is being redefined based on feelings. Cultural norms are being established based on feelings. And while that is dangerous in and of itself, it gets even more dangerous when we realize that feelings change. They can turn on a dime. Not only that, but feelings usually differ based on who you are and what perspective you have.

I have no doubt that the Cowboys fans all felt that Dak got in the end zone as they watched the replay angles. I also have no doubt that the Eagles fans felt as though Dak didn't. Any time you base your values, beliefs, and decisions on feelings, you are no longer basing them on the truth.

If I were to guess, you wouldn't fly on the plane, yield to the surgeon, or trust the pharmacist in my earlier examples, because when it comes to your life and health, you want people who know the truth and function based on it. You don't want people who are haggling or hustling. You want the truth. And yet, despite truth's importance in so many ways, we are living in a day when truth is dying all around us. Everything has been left to be defined by emotions, manipulation, propaganda, or agendas, which has led to cataclysmic confusion and chaos in myriad realms.

For starters, we are witnessing psychological chaos all around us. People's mental trajectory has gone astray because truth no longer serves as a baseline for the mind. We also see philosophical chaos as individuals and scholars doodle with ideas and theories ad nauseam. Scripture calls this ever learning yet never coming to the knowledge of the truth (2 Timothy 3:7). People collect information today like they used to collect trading cards or limited-edition Beanie Babies. It's amazing to me how people see a need to compile degree upon degree and yet often do not appear any brighter than when they began pursuing formal education. This is because they have often garnered these degrees at the graveyard of truth.

There is also scientific chaos as people deal with probabilities and possibilities only to discover that scientists seem to change their minds as frequently as the wind changes direction. Whether due to the discovery of new information or to different interpretations of existing data, rules based on science frequently have come across as nothing more than suggestions based on uncertainties. One year it is healthy to drink coffee; the next year it is not. One year it is healthy to eat bread, and the next it is not. These are mildly exaggerated examples, as I'm sure you are aware of the more personally impacting and life-influencing continual changes in science recently.

The continual changes, or even contradictory interpretations that can vary state by state, in our nation over the last few years have raised red flags for many of us. At times it even appears that rather than scientists defining themselves as "discoverers of truth," many have made the leap to seeking to be "determiners of truth"—even when that means reversing their own determinations quickly and frequently. This has led to division, chaos, confusion, and an overall hesitation in our culture to do what we have been asked to do—trust the science.

We are facing chaos in entertainment now too. Talk shows used to offer platforms for debating the topics of the day, but we now have nothing more than "babble by the hour." Confused people talk about confused ideals often rooted in one-sided perspectives, which then leads to an even more confused audience. There is no lack of opinions today, and it can be hard to distinguish who is telling the truth, whom you should believe, whom it is wise to follow, and from whom you need to learn. This leads to a cycle of friending and being friended, or unfriending and being unfriended, following and being followed, et cetera, based on what people say or don't say due to delusions about what is truth.

In addition to the mayhem in psychology, science, and entertainment, though, is the greatest cause of confusion in our land today: the existence of spiritual chaos. We now have crickets in the pulpit. Or we have a multitude of chirping. Or shouting. Or tickling of the ears. But what we don't have is clarity. What we don't have is truth. The one thing that ought to distinguish the Christian influencer or pastor, as well as the church of Jesus Christ, is that we are people of truth. We are people who take the concept of truth seriously. And yet even within much of the church today, truth has left the building.

Thus, when I set out to write a book on what our nation needs most right now—a return to Christian character and kingdom values—I realized I needed to start at the foundation where values are formed. Without a foundation of truth, character and values carry about as much weight and consistency as that wind I mentioned earlier. Change the definition of the truth, and by default, you'll have to change the values assigned to it, or rising from it. That's why the first part of this book will look at what truth is, where we find it, how we use it, and the ways we apply it. Truth is the foundation of character. Then, after we have studied truth and we understand its importance in our lives, the second part of the book will focus on the core kingdom values Jesus taught His disciples while seated on a mountainside I visited not too long ago, right next to the Sea of Galilee.

> **Without a foundation of truth, character and values carry about as much weight and consistency as the wind.**

I'll never forget the first time I stood on this mountainside where Jesus delivered His message known today as the Sermon on the Mount. What impacted me most was the sea. I had always thought that the sea Jesus had sent His disciples to cross the night they ran into the enormous storm was an enormous sea. But standing there on the mountainside that day during my first trip to Israel, I could clearly see to the other side of the water.

The story made a lot more sense to me once I knew the truth of the size of the sea, because in order for the disciples to be caught in a storm in the middle of it, the storm had to have come upon them very quickly. Sure, I had read in the Bible that the storm came upon them suddenly, but it wasn't until I actually saw the relatively small size of the sea that I realized the full truth of it. This helped me to understand more clearly how the disciples could have gotten into the boat, even if there were clouds brewing in the distance, and assumed they would make it safely to the other side. Truth has a way of bringing clarity to our understanding.

WHAT IS TRUTH?

Let's set the stage on our opening subject by looking at that iconic conversation between Jesus and Pilate found in John 18:33–38. In one of Jesus' last earthly conversations, we read,

> Therefore Pilate entered again into the Praetorium, and summoned Jesus and said to Him, "Are You the King of the Jews?" Jesus answered, "Are you saying this on your own initiative, or did others tell you about Me?" Pilate answered, "I am not a Jew, am I? Your own nation and the chief priests delivered You to me; what have You done?" Jesus answered, "My kingdom is not of this world. If My kingdom were of this world, then My servants would be fighting so that I would not be handed over to the Jews; but as it is, My kingdom is not of this realm." Therefore Pilate said to Him, "So You are a king?" Jesus answered, "You say correctly that I am a king. For this I have been born, and for this I have come into the world, to

15

testify to the truth. Everyone who is of the truth hears My voice." Pilate said to Him, "What is truth?"

What is truth? Pilate asked the question of our culture today when he spoke to Jesus on that day. He asked what we hear over and over again in arguments and disputes and especially online: What in the world is truth? And what's more, who defines it?

Granted, it's hard to know what truth is if you live in a culture that denies its existence. Pilate didn't live in a world of absolutes. He was an agnostic. He questioned whether anyone could know truth. But rather than pointing fingers at Pilate, if we open our eyes in our Christian culture today, we can find many people exactly like him.

Far too many believers question whether truth exists. The concept of truth has become one for debate in and of itself. Some lean more toward rationalism, which means that truth is what a person can intellectually perceive or learn. For rationalists, truth is that which your mind can grab in such a way that it makes sense to you.

Other people tend toward pragmatism. Pragmatism defines truth more in line with what works. If something works at that point in time, then it must be truth for that point in time. Still others lean toward world views in which truth is subjective; it's more about how you feel or what you choose to believe. Truth becomes nothing more than "my truth," "your truth," "his truth," or "her truth." Relativism and postmodernism call truth according to the way reality is viewed by each person (relativism), or even how each person would prefer to view it (postmodernism).

Essentially, we are living in a world of *isms*, each seeking to define truth according to its own theories, goals, and agendas. But Jesus didn't mince words when He said in verse 37, "And for this I have come into the world, to testify to the truth." Jesus didn't hold truth up for debate. Jesus told Pilate, as well as anyone else who has ears to hear Him, that He is the one who testifies to the truth.

Truth can be defined as an absolute standard by which reality is measured. Jesus tells us not only that truth exists but also that it is a powerful force when He states in John 8:32, "And you will know the truth, and the truth will make you free." Truth is not a made-up concept. Truth exists. Jesus testifies to its existence and says that you and I can come to know truth for ourselves.

This absolute and objective standard by which reality is measured sits outside of you and me. Because of that, truth transcends emotions. How you feel does not determine whether something is true. Last time I checked, one plus one equals two. That truth does not rest on whether you feel that it equals two. It does not depend on whether you wish that it would equal three. The truth is that one plus one always equals two. Regardless of how you feel about something that is true, you need to keep in mind that your feelings don't determine the truth. Your feelings could be wrong. Truth does not need your emotions to approve it or validate it. One plus one has always equaled two, and it will always equal two. This is because it is a fixed absolute standard by which reality is to be measured. Without this standard, much of what rests on mathematical formulas and programs would come crashing to a halt. Without this standard, the physics of the universe would collapse, as would the world in which we live.

Don't you want to know when you get on an airplane that the truth of gravity always works as an absolute standard? Doesn't it give you both confidence and comfort to know that gravity doesn't deviate based on how people feel? You wouldn't want to fly if gravity were a negotiable standard that sometimes worked as stated and at other times didn't. What's more, you certainly want to know when you get on an airplane that the truth of aerodynamics always works too. Why? Because without it, your plane will crash on takeoff.

Our society is not as opposed to truth as many may make it out to be. Nearly all of us operate on a foundation of truth in many sectors of our lives. Yet when it comes to our own identity and personal character qualities as human beings, that's where truth seems to be tossed straight out the window.

The climate in our culture reminds me of a conversation I once had with my dad. He was older and was struggling with a sickness. When I asked him if the medication the doctor had prescribed was helping him, he replied, "No." When I asked why, he told me that he didn't like that medicine.

"So what did you do, Dad?" I asked him.

"I changed doctors," he responded.

Too many people today are changing pastors, teachers, news outlets, social media influencers, authors, and even friends when someone says something they don't like or with which they disagree. Cancel culture has taken on a whole new level in that I have even seen families cancel each other over disagreements on what they believe to be true. What we've got today are people bouncing around until they find somebody who will tell them what they want to hear.

A professor told his class one day that they were going to start off the year with his opening philosophical statement, "There are no absolutes." The professor went on to share that you cannot come to a fixed position on anything at all. One of the students in the professor's class raised his hand after the professor had finished making his introductory remarks. The student sought to clarify that the professor had just said there are no absolutes.

Once the professor affirmed this to the student, the student paused, then followed up with a question: "Professor, are you absolutely sure?"

While this isn't a true story, you can imagine the laughter in the room if it were. The professor had postulated an absolute by stating that there are none. You must decide, as every Christian should, where you stand on this subject of truth. Now, I didn't say you must decide what is truth. Rather, you must decide where you stand on the matter of truth. You must decide if you are going to fall sway to a culture that allows each person to do what is right in their own eyes (Judges 21:25), or if you are going to recognize that there is an objective standard by which truth has been established. Contaminated and sinful flesh cannot be relied upon to establish or maintain truth. Sinfulness distorts the truth. Trust rests in the pure perfection of the Creator himself.

Another reason why humanity cannot serve as our own standard for truth is because we are finite. We are limited. We don't know all things about all things. This is why we learn. This is why we study. This is why we change our minds as we discover information.

What's more, that which we learn from isn't always rooted in truth. Sometimes we find out later in our journey that what we were learning and believing to be true were lies, misinformation, or propaganda. By the way, this isn't anything new. This stems from what is known as "doctrines of demons" (1 Timothy 4:1).

Demons have a school in which most of humanity has enrolled over the years. Satan and his demonic forces seek to trick people with half-truths, partial truths, and all-out lies to deceive and control the population. I would imagine that there is not one person reading this book who has not been duped by the devil at one time or another. Satan is the father of lies, and he's a master at deceptions, particularly those cloaked in partial truths. It's far easier to swallow a lie that's coated in truth. The devil knows that, which is why you'll often find truth mixed in with lies when he sets out to deceive (Genesis 3:1–6; Matthew 4:1–11).

You and I are living in a worldwide web of lies. Everywhere we look and everywhere we go, we are bombarded with secular billboards blasting lies. Sure, they might be nicely painted, dressed up, and sophisticated-sounding lies, but they are still lies. We live in a land of duplicity that has increasingly drifted away from a Judeo-Christian ethic, ultimately washing ashore onto a liar's paradise. The devil is deceitful, so the culture is contaminated.

If you want to discover absolute truth from which kingdom values arise, it must come from an absolute Source. Perfect truth comes only out of a perfect Source. Everything else is guesswork.

And there is only one perfect Source in the universe: God.

This is why many political movements such as socialism, communism, and Marxism seek to keep religion either eradicated or marginalized. That way they don't have to deal with an absolute. They don't have to deal with God. Leaders in those systems want government to be the arbiter of truth. Even in our own nation, as we shift away from a Judeo-Christian world view, there has been an increased attack on the freedom of religion. This is because without God, there is no truth. God is truth. We read it time and again in Scripture (emphasis added):

- ▸ "Into Your hand I commit my spirit; You have ransomed me, O Lord, **God of truth**" (Psalm 31:5).
- ▸ "Because he who is blessed in the earth will be blessed by the **God of truth**; and he who swears in the earth will swear by the **God of truth**; because the former troubles are forgotten, and because they are hidden from My sight!" (Isaiah 65:16).
- ▸ "So that by two unchangeable things in which it is **impossible for God to lie**, we who have taken refuge would have strong encouragement to take hold of the hope set before us" (Hebrews 6:18).
- ▸ "May it never be! Rather, let **God be found true**, though every man be found a liar, as it is written, 'That You may be justified in Your words, and prevail when You are judged'" (Romans 3:4).

When you, or people you know, disagree with God, then you (or they) are wrong. It is impossible for God to be wrong. God is truth. There are two answers to every question—God's answer and everybody else's. And when everybody else disagrees with God, then everybody else is wrong.

There is nothing in God's nature that even makes it possible for Him to lie. He knows everything about everything. And when you know everything about everything, you can't be wrong. When you know the past, present, and future, you can't be wrong. When you are the one who made it all to begin with, who sustains it all in every moment, you can't be wrong. Jesus declared that as a part of the triune Godhead, He came "full of grace and truth" (John 1:14).

He also boldly stated in John 14:6, "I am the way, and the truth, and the life; no one comes to the Father but through Me." Notice, Jesus did not say that He is *a* way or *a* truth. He said He is *the* way and *the* truth. Jesus is not just one among many. He is *the* standard by which truth is to be measured.

In addition, the Bible calls the Holy Spirit, the third member of the Trinity, "the Spirit of truth" (John 14:17; 15:26; 16:13). The Holy Spirit transfers the truth of God to us so that we can know the way to go and the decisions to make. He serves as our Teacher, Instructor, and Guide.

God is truth.

Jesus is truth.

The Holy Spirit is truth.

Thus, truth is whatever God has declared it to be. Truth is not what the latest opinion poll says. It's not what the surveys say. It's not what the journalists report. It's not what the pundits push. All of that is secondary to what God has spoken on a subject. And, by the way, God has spoken on every subject. You may need to study some to find out what He has to say, but He has spoken.

Truth is never sourced in this world order. Truth is always sourced in God alone. It comes from another realm because He comes from another realm. Truth sits outside of time and space. It also sits outside of our five senses. Truth cannot be determined in human terms because its Originator and Author is not human.

That's why the overarching question you should be asking yourself on every single subject you study or learn about is this: What has God said on the matter? If you ask that on the front end instead of the back, you will save yourself a lot time and consequences.

An airplane pilot needs a control tower because the pilot cannot see everything. There might be something coming up that the pilot needs to know about ahead of time. Or the pilot may need to be alerted to other planes in the vicinity. That's why a pilot needs something outside of himself or herself—whether that is the control tower or the radar—to guide the plane safely through the sky. Similarly, you and I need a control tower. We need something or Someone outside of us—bigger than we are—Someone who can see beyond what we can see to guide us through this life.

> The overarching question you should be asking yourself on every single subject you study or learn about is this: What has God said on the matter?

God is our guide.

We live in a world that camouflages lies with truth. It's like the man who came home from a fishing trip and showed his wife twenty huge fish. She was very impressed. "You caught all of those?" she asked.

"Oh yeah, I caught them all," he replied, grinning from ear to ear.

The problem was the wife knew her husband, and his fishing skills, too well. So she asked again, "Now, before God, you really did catch those?"

He responded, "Well, yes. I went to the fish market after my trip and told the fishmonger to throw each one to me. So yeah, I caught them!"

Was what he had originally said a fact? Yes, it was a fact. He had caught all twenty fish. But was it true? Not at all.

See, what the world does is it tells you facts, but it does not tell you the truth. Facts without truth are just another way of lying.

The question you and I need to answer for ourselves as we go on this journey of kingdom values is who are we going to look to as the source of truth? Will it be our friends? Will it be the academics? Scholars? Preachers? Social media influencers? Media? Politicians? Moral instincts? Our own feelings, hopes, or desires? Or will it be the true Source: God himself? In order to have shared kingdom values as a culture or society, we will have to look to the same Source for truth: God. He is the standard by which all else is measured.

I have a family member who lives in England, and when I have gone to visit over the years, one of the sights we usually go see is Big Ben. It towers over the other buildings nearby, offering the precise standard for time. In fact, I've seen men in three-piece suits pull out their pocket watch or check their wristwatch and then look up at Big Ben. What they are doing is looking up to the source of the most accurate time in order to synchronize their own watch with it.

Now, if someone's pocket watch differs from Big Ben, you see them adjust their pocket watch. You don't see them climb up the tower to adjust Big Ben. Big Ben doesn't adjust to anyone. When the people's watches differ, then it is the people's watches that must be adjusted.

Likewise, when it comes to our lives and decisions, God wants us to look to Him as the source of what is true. He doesn't want us to look to what our parents said, what the professors said, our friends, the news, or anything else. When what we think or feel differs from what God says, it is what we think or feel that needs to adjust—not God. God is truth.

As our culture descends into greater chaos with each passing day, it is high time for those of us who claim the name of Jesus Christ to return to the truth. We are not to apologize for being people of the truth. We ought to live with an unwavering commitment to the absolute, divinely authorized objective standard by which reality is to be measured. When you and I do that, when we live as people of the truth, we will bring calm to the chaos that surrounds us.

As kingdom followers of Jesus Christ, we are supposed to make an imprint on earth from the influence of heaven. We are to pray like Jesus, "Thy kingdom come, Thy will be done in earth, as it is in heaven" (Matthew 6:10 KJV). We are to live according to the truth because that is the only way we will fully invite God's healing hope and intervention into the cultural chaos that seeks to engulf us.

There's a story of a ship that had headed down a waterway on a foggy evening. It was a very treacherous waterway, and the captain could barely see anything in front of him. This was in the days before the high-tech instruments captains have now. All the captain could do to navigate the waterway was to look out ahead and steer as best he could.

However, as he looked ahead, there appeared to be a light. The captain assumed the light to be an oncoming boat, so he sent the captain of the other boat a message, "Go three degrees north so that we do not crash."

The message came back to him, "No, you go three degrees south so that there is no crash."

The captain was irritated at the reply, so he sent his own command again. "I told you, go three degrees north so that we do not collide!"

The message came back again, "No, you go three degrees south so there is no collision!"

The captain then tried to pull rank. He said, "I am a captain. I am an officer in the US Navy, and I demand that you go three degrees north!"

The message came back, "I am a lighthouse. I do not move."

Let's stop negotiating with God as if we outrank Him. He is the truth. He does not move. We must adjust to the truth and live as people of truth if we are to avoid the personal chaos, crashes, and collisions so prevalent around us.

2

THE ATTACK ON TRUTH

Juneteenth is a significant holiday for many people because it is a day set aside to recognize and celebrate the end of slavery in the United Sates. The Emancipation Proclamation was signed on January 1, 1863, to legally end the system of enslavement. But most people don't realize that it took two more years for many slaves to find out they were free. Juneteenth occurred on June 19, 1865, when two thousand Union troops came to Galveston Bay and set free 250,000 slaves who were still operating under the old system of slavery.

Even though for two and a half years these individuals were legally free, they behaved as though they were enslaved because they didn't know they were not. The Confederate soldiers were still holding territory there, and they refused to yield to the proclamation made by President Lincoln in 1863. It took another power backed by several thousand soldiers to bring to reality what had been established legally.

There exists another kind of slavery today that holds people hostage. It keeps them chained to an existence outside of their own spiritual desires. It is the slavery Jesus addresses in John 8:31–32: "So Jesus was saying to those Jews who had believed Him, 'If you continue in My word, then you are truly disciples of Mine; and you will know the truth, and the truth will make you free.'"

Jesus was speaking to people who believed in Him. They were already Christians, already His followers. Yet despite knowing Jesus, accepting Him, and loving Him, they still needed to be set free. See, you can know Jesus and even spend time with Jesus but still be bound in traps of the enemy.

When a person trusts in Christ alone for the forgiveness of their sins, they are saved for eternity, but freedom on earth from sin's strangleholds is a process. Salvation does not automatically remove all of the ropes and chains that once held a person hostage. To be set free means to be released from something that ought not to be shackling or limiting you anymore. To live free is to experience the full expression of your destiny in this life. But freedom is only accessed through truth, and truth has gone missing—as we have previously seen.

Because truth is often nowhere to be found, far too many people find themselves illegitimately confined as spiritual prisoners of war. They are locked behind enemy lines, unable to break the chains that bind them. The reason this happens so frequently on earth is because our freedom is opposed by a very powerful force. We face an enemy who would like nothing more than to keep each of us trapped in a sticky web of lies.

We gain a greater glimpse into this enemy a few verses down from what we just read in John 8, where Jesus reveals him clearly:

"Why do you not understand what I am saying? It is because you cannot hear My word. You are of your father the devil, and you want to do the desires of your father. He was a murderer from the beginning and does not stand in the truth because there is no truth in him. Whenever he speaks a lie, he speaks from his own nature, for he is a liar and the father of lies. But because I speak the truth, you do not believe Me."

vv. 43–45

Jesus boldly states here that Satan is nothing but a liar. Everything about the devil is clothed in deception. What's more, he's been lying all through the ages. To help us understand Satan's reasoning for twisting truth and telling lies, we need to look at his overarching agenda. His purpose is revealed to us in Isaiah 14:12–14. It says,

> "How you have fallen from heaven, O star of the morning, son of the dawn! You have been cut down to the earth, you who have weakened the nations! But you said in your heart, 'I will ascend to heaven; I will raise my throne above the stars of God, and I will sit on the mount of assembly in the recesses of the north. I will ascend above the heights of the clouds; I will make myself like the Most High.'"

In this passage we quickly see that Satan's one goal is to build a kingdom that rivals God's. His bottom-line agenda is to usurp God's rightful rule and authority. We know this by what he said. Phrases like "I will ascend," and "I will raise," and "I will sit," and "I will make myself like the Most High" reveal his endgame. Satan was jealous of God from the start. So his motivation is to be like God himself. He wants the glory, the attention, and the control.

It appears to me, as I read those verses, that Satan wanted his independence. He didn't want to have to answer to a higher rule. He wanted to call the shots. To be the chief in charge. He also wanted to have all eyes on him, worshiping him as all of creation once worshiped God.

In order to achieve his aim, Satan set in motion a process of deception. As a result of his propaganda and lies, he got one-third of all the angels to follow him. Keep in mind, these were sinless angels. That's an important point because if sinless angels could be deceived to follow the devil, we probably shouldn't think for even a minute that you or I can outmaneuver him. He's very good at his craft, and his lies often come half-baked in truths, making it difficult to discern what is true.

When God created humanity, He gave the well-known instruction to Adam that he was not to eat of the Tree of Knowledge of Good and Evil (Genesis 2:17). It was the one forbidden action. God gave Adam a lush garden filled with all manner of delicious fruit, but He forbade him to eat off of what I like to call the "Google tree." I refer to it as that because the tree was an information source that would open up a Pandora's box of thoughts.

> Truth must originate from the Source, or it becomes convoluted in iterations that send humanity down rabbit holes of hopelessness based on a plethora of lies.

The tree had been put there to let Adam know he was not the one to determine what is good or what is evil, independently of God. God was to be Adam's information center. God was to be his Google search engine. God was to be the definition of what is right and what is wrong. Truth must originate from the Source, or it becomes convoluted in iterations that send humanity down rabbit holes of hopelessness based on a plethora of lies.

The beginning of nearly all of these lies starts with Satan's go-to line, "Has God said?" He begins his deception with Adam and Eve by raising a question about the integrity of God.

Does God really know what He is talking about?

Is God really informed?

Does God really understand you?

Does God really want what is best for you?

Can God really figure you out?

Does God really care?

The questions can change, but their root remains the same. Satan seeks to strip away any belief in the integrity of God that he can. He sought to do that with Adam and Eve, and he seeks to do the same with us today. He does this by making it look like God is gaming everyone. That God isn't really telling the truth. He does this by trying to make us believe that we are being played. And no one wants to be played.

This isn't just a scheme confined by the walls of a garden, though. This is a global scheme that has unfolded throughout history. First John 5:19 says, "The whole world lies in the power of the evil one." The whole world. This is a large-scale global attack of deception (see Revelation 12:9). The same way Satan successfully deceived Adam and Eve thousands of years ago is how he is seeking to do the same to us right now. He hasn't changed his approach. Why would he? It still works.

PLANTING THOUGHTS LIKE SEEDS

What Satan did to Eve was bring a thought to her mind. A question. As in the popular movie *Inception*, he planted a thought like a seed. And before long, she began to think it was her own thought. But please notice, the thought did not come from her. The thought came from the devil, who introduced the thought to her. He planted his question on God's integrity into her thinking in such a way that it seemed to Eve that it was her question.

As a result, this one thought changed how she saw the world around her. It changed her perspective, her world view. It changed her mindset. We discover this in Genesis 3:6: "The woman saw that the tree was good for food, and that it was a delight to the eyes, and that the tree was desirable to make one wise."

Don't forget that Eve had been seeing this tree every day. This was not the first time she saw it. But after having Satan's deceptive thoughts planted in her mind, she saw the tree differently—from a new vantage point. The tree was no longer a symbol of obedience to and respect for the Creator of the universe, God; it was now "desirable to make one wise." She desired the tree for what it supposedly could give her.

Her thought had erupted into a desire that caused her to doubt the integrity of her Creator. The result was disobedience. Satan had used deception to lead to doubt, which turned into desire, which culminated in disobedience.

That's his same game plan for today. This is why, before we examine anything related to kingdom virtues, we have to understand the extent of the war on truth. We have to identify the Source of truth. Otherwise, anyone can say that anything is a virtue or character quality. I'm sure Satan made it seem to Eve as though gaining information was a good value or character quality. That's how she was deceived. The devil didn't frame it as what it was—disobedience. He framed the sin as a positive, a desire for knowledge.

Because of Satan's clever distortions of values, we need to first realize that whatever character quality we are to have, teach, model, and reflect to a watching world must stem from the true Source. If it doesn't, it will not be a true kingdom value. Sure, it might look good in the moment, but at best you'll wind up not with true virtue, but with virtue signaling.

And isn't that what we have a lot of these days? It seems there is an uptick in the number of people seeking to appear virtuous in what they do or say, but then we find out later, through some scandal or another, that it was all a charade. Virtue signaling is not virtue. In fact, virtue signaling is most often rooted in pride, which makes it a sin. God is opposed to pride.

When Adam and Eve sinned against God by living according to their own newly defined virtue of knowledge seeking and awareness, their whole world collapsed. The environment collapsed. The ground—once rich soil and foliage—became full of thorns and thistles. Their relationship collapsed, putting them at odds with each other. Their family would go on to collapse with one son killing the other. Their peace collapsed as childbearing now came with great pain. And their future collapsed as they faced an end date to what had previously been a continual existence.

In a football game, if one player commits a foul, the whole team is penalized. That's just how it works. The whole team suffers. Similarly, when Adam sinned, the whole world fell into chaos. What's true with Adam holds true today in many ways—sin has a way of affecting much more than those people and things in the immediate circle of the sinner. Satan knows the impact of sin and its far-reaching effects. That's why he is so persistent at planting seeds to displace the root of truth in a person's life.

The goal of deception is to keep you away from God. The longer you believe the lies, the longer you live apart from God's abiding presence with you, as well as the divine assistance He makes available to you. This is because God cannot partner with or participate in a lie.

Now, lies come in all shapes and sizes. Even the Antichrist will go on to perform great miracles and signs with false wonders (2 Thessalonians 2:1–10). A person can be tricked with things that seem good. Have you ever heard the phrase *too good to be true*? Just because something is a miracle doesn't mean it is from God. That's why we are told in 1 John 4:1–3 to "test the spirits" in order to determine and discern which is from God. Just because someone or something sounds good doesn't mean it is or they are good. Satan is very clever at knowing exactly how to trip you up. He has the playbook on all of us in order to go after our personal weaknesses.

The chaos in our culture today and the societal calamities we face globally are due to the majority of people on this planet watering the seeds of the lies from the devil. Satan's deception creates confusion as he seeks to redefine what it means to be a man, a woman, or a family. What it means to be a certain race or ethnicity. What it means to be popular or valuable or even significant. Even what it means to be attractive. Satan subtly erodes the fiber of our future by redefining what it means to have character. He doesn't want you or me living according to the values of the kingdom of light. He wants you and me to embrace his values from his kingdom of darkness. So he seeks to deceive each of us in our own ways, knowing that what will work with one person may not work with another.

Let me go back to football for just a second. When a football team gets ready to play a game, they will do a lot of things to prepare for their opponent. One thing you can count on a team *always* doing is reviewing the game film of their opponent. By looking at the game film, they are seeking to ascertain the other team's tendencies and weaknesses. They want to discern what motivates them to act, or react, as they do. In studying the enemy, they gain a better grasp of how to defeat the enemy.

Now, while Satan may come at you like your friend—promising you pleasure, notoriety, fame, family, or friends—there is one thing you need to realize from the start: Satan is not on your side. Satan is your enemy. He hates you. He is the opponent. And the reason he hates you so much is because you are made in the image of the One he hates most: God.

Sure, Satan may sweet-talk you sometimes, but his strategy is always to take you out. Thus, like a football team preparing to face an opponent, Satan studies you. He studies your game film. He digs through the clips to discover what motivates you, triggers you, and causes you to act or react in a way that he wants. In studying you—in studying each of us—the devil and his demons know which strings to pull and which buttons to push. It's not the same strategy for every believer. No, Satan's got your number and uniquely zeroes in on what it takes to trip you up from living a life marked by kingdom character.

Because Satan and his minions have studied you and know you so well, they will be consistent in bringing to you the snares into which you are most apt to fall. Sometimes they are presented in the creation of false doctrines or false rules, at other times through someone who opposes true doctrine and truth-based virtues. We read about what Satan does, as well as what our response should be, in 1 Timothy 4:

> But the Spirit explicitly says that in later times some will fall away from the faith, paying attention to deceitful spirits and doctrines of

demons, by means of the hypocrisy of liars seared in their own conscience as with a branding iron, men who forbid marriage and advocate abstaining from foods which God has created to be gratefully shared in by those who believe and know the truth. For everything created by God is good, and nothing is to be rejected if it is received with gratitude; for it is sanctified by means of the word of God and prayer. In pointing out these things to the brethren, you will be a good servant of Christ Jesus, constantly nourished on the words of the faith and of the sound doctrine which you have been following.

vv. 1–6

Deceitful spirits and demons prey on those who live inauthentic, hypocritical lives. They prey on those who have had their own conscience seared as with a branding iron. They prey on those who have lived far enough away from the truth that they no longer even recognize it. And the way they get those who still discern the truth into a position where their conscience no longer works is through a subtle steering away in small increments, as Satan did to Eve when he questioned, "Has God said?"

Paul addresses this in 2 Corinthians 11:3 when he warns his readers, "But I am afraid that, as the serpent deceived Eve by his craftiness, your minds will be led astray from the simplicity and purity of devotion to Christ." Paul makes it clear what our key virtue as believers ought to

> Deceitful spirits and demons prey on those who have lived far enough away from the truth that they no longer even recognize it.

be in this statement. We are to be purely devoted to Jesus Christ. This is why so much of what you witness in the world today works as a distraction from such devotion.

Have you ever sat down to pray, only to have every person in your contact list text you all at the same time? That's an exaggeration, but you know what I mean. It seems that whenever we choose to spend time with Jesus Christ, something else comes up to try to lure us away. Paul explains why and through whom this happens several verses later in 2 Corinthians 11:13–15. He writes,

> For such men are false apostles, deceitful workers, disguising themselves as apostles of Christ. No wonder, for even Satan disguises himself as an angel of light. Therefore it is not surprising if his servants also disguise themselves as servants of righteousness, whose end will be according to their deeds.

Satan's strategy is simple: He wants to mess with your mind. And he doesn't mind dressing up as an angel of light to do that. That's how we wind up with so many people willing to give up their lives to cult leaders, from Waco to Guyana, or wherever. It's because people's minds have been hijacked by "deceitful workers, disguising themselves as apostles of Christ." Satan doesn't always (and might never) wear a red jumpsuit and carry a pitchfork. But he does know many ways to make himself and his demons appear in an appealing, attractive, and alluring way. This false light then confuses those who do not know the truth of God enough to discern fact from fiction.

We have public schools, and even some Christian schools, drawing kids away from the truth these days. We have television programs and movies entertaining people away from the truth. We've got racial leaders destroying people's lives by taking a legitimate subject and convoluting it so deeply with lies that they are pulling people away from the truth. We've even got pastors and so-called spiritual leaders painting a new version of faith that allows for anything and everything to be considered the truth.

The only way to identify a lie is to know the truth. But if a person does not know the truth, the lies will consume him or her. And before you know it, not only will this person be accepting lies as truth, but they will be endorsing them. That's how deep Satan's deception runs. He's clever. He will get a person to die for a lie while condemning and criticizing those who are standing for the truth.

It reminds me of the farmer who had gotten tired of the neighborhood boys coming and stealing his watermelons. After enough times, he decided he would be clever about how he handled it. The farmer decided to put up a sign at the edge of his watermelon garden that read "One of these watermelons is poisoned." *That'll do it*, the farmer thought, as he wedged his freshly painted sign into the ground.

The problem was that the farmer underestimated the neighborhood boys. When he came out the next day, he saw that the word *one* had been crossed out with red paint. In its place was painted the word *two*. The farmer lost his whole crop because he could not outwit the thieves seeking to do him harm.

OUR WEAPONS AGAINST THE ENEMY

Satan is a thief who wants nothing more than to do you harm. If you think you are going to somehow outsmart him, outmaneuver him, or outwit him, I advise you to think again. This isn't his first rodeo, and you aren't his first prey. Satan has been doing this too long. That's why the only way you are going to uncover his lies in your life and reveal his plan to take you down is by taking every thought you have captive to the Word of God. You are to study God's Word and discern what God says on the matter. That should be your first question on every subject: What does God say about it?

Let me remind you: Satan is not on your side. Siding with Satan and his alterations of truth in order to fit comfortably in contemporary culture is the worst thing a believer can do. Satan is a roaring lion hunting for his next meal (1 Peter 5:8). We read about his intentions in Revelation 12:7–10, where it says,

> And there was war in heaven, Michael and his angels waging war with the dragon. The dragon and his angels waged war, and they were not strong enough, and there was no longer a place found for them in heaven. And the great dragon was thrown down, the serpent of old

who is called the devil and Satan, who deceives the whole world; he was thrown down to the earth, and his angels were thrown down with him. Then I heard a loud voice in heaven, saying, "Now the salvation, and the power, and the kingdom of our God and the authority of His Christ have come, for the accuser of our brethren has been thrown down, he who accuses them before our God day and night."

Satan is the accuser. This is a legal term. Satan's role in this case for humanity is to act as the prosecuting attorney seeking to bring judgment on everyone he can. When we sin, he has evidence against us because we have disobeyed God. The purpose of condemning us is to legitimize righteous judgment against us for our betrayal of God. That's his goal. Satan's goal is to get you to use your own free will to choose to disobey God.

But in the next verse, the author of Revelation goes on to tell us how we are to overcome him: "And they overcame him because of the blood of the Lamb and because of the word of their testimony, and they did not love their life even when faced with death" (v. 11). You and I are to overcome Satan through the blood of Jesus and the word of our testimony. Satan can be beaten in court. But that is only due to the advocate we have in Jesus Christ. First John 2:1–2 says it like this:

And if anyone sins, we have an Advocate with the Father, Jesus Christ the righteous; and He Himself is the propitiation for our sins; and not for ours only, but also for those of the whole world.

Jesus is our defense attorney. What's more, He works pro bono (without a fee) because the price has already been paid on the cross. When Satan takes you to court to accuse you, rather than bow before the reality of what you have done, know that Jesus Christ has already overcome sin. You have an Advocate who is also the Judge's Son. Appeal to Him, His forgiveness, and His call to live the rest of your life as a kingdom disciple who models kingdom virtues out of a heart of pure devotion to Jesus Christ.

When you appeal to the sacrifice of Jesus Christ, which paid the penalty for your sin, you are telling the accuser that the accusation has already been covered. It might be real, but it is no longer relevant. By confessing through the word of your testimony to the power of Jesus Christ, you are acting as a person on the stand bearing witness to the power of the truth.

As you bring up the truth of God's Word before the many issues you may face, Satan will have to retreat. He holds no power or authority over God. In fact, Satan is allergic to Scripture because he's allergic to truth. Like the Wicked Witch of the West, who was destroyed by water in *The Wizard of Oz*, Satan dissolves in the presence of truth. He flees when you call on the blood of Jesus through the power of your testimony rooted in the basic building block of truth in God's Word. Now that we've uncovered his agenda and strategy, as well as our strategy for defeating him, let's look at why we must defeat him.

Have you ever played the game truth or dare? It's a popular game with teens and young adults. In this game, each player gets to choose whether they will answer a question truthfully or accept a dare instead. Both choices are risky if a person has something to hide. This is why a lot of people wind up choosing a dare.

Unfortunately, our culture has a lot to hide these days. There are many secrets stuffed in the closets of our souls. Truth is absent not only from the world but oftentimes from our own lives as well. So turn after turn, we keep choosing a dare in this game of life. However, God sets the rules in this game. And a dare always comes with a consequence. Since a dare goes against God's standards and His way of operating, we find ourselves facing consequences stacked on each other. This results in the development of bad character, for which we need to repent.

We'll learn more about this and about why it is sometimes difficult to spot the real reason for the difficulties we face in our lives in the next chapter.

3

THE ABSENCE OF TRUTH

One of the major political, social, racial, and cultural issues of the day is the issue of voter suppression. The concern voiced by those who advocate for greater accessibility for voters is that they believe there are influences that intentionally seek to limit or deny equal access to the ballot box. Obviously, equal access is one of the hallmarks of a democracy. Because of this, the battle rages in various communities and states in the quest to provide ample opportunities for voting among all people.

However, there is a greater suppression we face today, with implications much deeper and consequences that last much longer than the suppression of a vote—as important as that issue is. It is the suppression of truth in our culture at large. When a culture suppresses truth—or even seeks to cancel it—it will leave lasting negative results in everything. It leads to errant character, resulting in expanding cultural chaos.

Whether in the name of popularity, preference, independence, or political correctness, we are facing a season in our society when truth has become suppressed. What's more, we are paying the price for this suppression. Romans 1:18 summarizes it like this:

For the wrath of God is revealed from heaven against all ungodliness and unrighteousness of men who suppress the truth in
unrighteousness.

To suppress something means to hold it down. To suppress is
to restrict, limit, or even not allow something to be what it was
designed to be or to do what it was designed to do. I'm sure you've
been to a beach or a swimming pool and seen an inflated ball suppressed beneath the water for a time. Because of the air in the ball, it
is designed to float on the water. But when it is held under—forced
down against what it is designed to do—and then let go, it will
explode to the surface, causing a bit of chaos.

Something similar is happening in our world today, especially
in our nation. We call it *cancel culture*. This culture is one in which
people or viewpoints that you do not like or agree with, or that
you prefer not spread, are squashed, hindered, limited—canceled.
Cancel culture is a form of suppression. It is limiting another person's freedom to believe and say something different from what
society has deemed acceptable to believe or say. When applied to
Christian subjects or Christian viewpoints, as it is regularly, it falls
within the classification of what Paul called in Romans 1:18 the
suppression of truth.

Now, you can't actually hold truth down against its will for too
long, just as you can't hold the inflated ball under the water indefi-
nitely unless you tether it. This is because the nature of truth is to
be true—to float above the surface of our hearts and our minds so
we can recognize it for what it is. The goal of truth is never to hide,
be dismissed, or be marginalized. And yet our culture seeks to force
it down, deny it, reject it, limit it, and compromise it in order to
remove it from the equation.

Paul explains that this suppression of truth exists because humanity wants its own way independent of God. Paul tells us that
the reason people seek to suppress truth is simply due to "unrighteousness." It is due to ungodliness. Humanity doesn't want God's

viewpoint. People don't want God's way. They don't want God to have a say in their thoughts, actions, or even character. Thus, truth has been kicked to the curb. It's been kicked out of our schools. It's been booted out of our government. It's been stripped from families. It's been pulled from relationships. Unfortunately, it's even been asked to leave the church at times.

I'm sure we have all been there at some point in time—in a situation where we didn't like what was being said, even though we knew it to be true. So we dismissed it, ignored it, or denied it. We suppressed the truth. Maybe that was you as a teenager, when your parents urged you to do what was right. We all know kids, teens, or young adults who seem to do this regularly in response to what their parents or other authorities say. They suppress the truth because the truth is not what they want to hear.

But just because you don't agree with something doesn't mean it is no longer true. James 4:12 states that only One exists as the ultimate decider of truth. We read, "There is only one Lawgiver and Judge, the One who is able to save and to destroy; but who are you who judge your neighbor?" Truth has an absolute Source. That Source is God. God is the only One who can absolutely know everything about everything at every moment in time.

YOU CAN'T HANDLE THE TRUTH

One of my all-time favorite movies is *A Few Good Men*. Most people who have seen the film remember the epic scene as the movie rolls to its conclusion. Tom Cruise's character is interrogating Jack Nicholson's on the stand. They intently stare each other down as their passions rise. When Nicholson asks, "You want answers?" Cruise yells in reply, "I want the truth!"

That's when Jack Nicholson looks him in the eyes and replies, "You can't handle the truth."*

A Few Good Men, directed by Rob Reiner (Columbia Pictures Industries, Inc., and Castle Rock Entertainment, 1992).

It seems that is where we have landed in our culture today. Everybody claims they want truth, in some form or fashion. But when truth comes to the surface, most people can't handle it. That's why a call for truth becomes little more than a call for consensus these days. It is a call for what the culture will deem true, or the ruling influencers will deem true—until that changes directions, and another call for consensus goes out.

The problem is that truth isn't created by consensus, and what's more, the lack of truth comes with consequences. If and when a culture chooses to suppress truth, that culture will face the consequences of its own choices. Essentially, the blame is on us. The reason God's wrath rains down can be found in Romans 1:19. We read that God unleashes His wrath "because that which is known about God is evident within them; for God made it evident to them." To put it as a parent would, we should know better than that. God has made truth evident to us. To suppress it is to deny its reality.

Everyone is born with a conscience. We have been given a truth regulator, a smoke detector of the soul. Our conscience knows the truth. Similarly, our conscience knows the smoke and mirrors of a lie. That's why you have probably found yourself innately knowing when something, or someone, is wrong, off, or shady. You know this because you are built with a conscience tied to truth.

The suppression of truth, over time, dulls the conscience. Like a smoke detector with depleted batteries, the dulled conscience becomes less and less activated or alert. Before you know it, a person's conscience can be buried so deep under a pile of lies that the person can no longer distinguish between truth and fiction, right and wrong. Such a conscience no longer works, and the result is the destruction of the character of a person or group of people.

Before this happens, though, we all have equal access to a conscience that helps us know the truth. Romans 2:15 explains that our conscience has been given to us to bear witness to what we do and say. It says,

They show the work of the Law written in their hearts, their conscience bearing witness and their thoughts alternately accusing or else defending them.

You might want to read that again. It's eye-opening. See, your conscience ought to make you feel guilty when you think or do something contrary to the truth. It also ought to make you feel confirmed when you think or do something that aligns with the truth.

If you have ever continued in a practice of sin, you'll know the cycle your conscience goes through. You will start off feeling guilty. But as you continue to move ahead with whatever sinful thought or action you are taking part in, you are suppressing the truth in your own life. You are holding down the manifestation of the truth. You might begin by making excuses. You dismiss any thoughts that you should stop. Yet eventually your conscience gets so used to what you are doing that you don't need excuses or dismissals anymore. In fact, your conscience becomes so dulled that it no longer even alerts you to your wrongdoing.

Your conscience started out as a gift from God to serve as a regulator for your human heart. It's a gift that has been given to everyone. That's why even if a person doesn't have a Bible or doesn't attend church—even if they are not a Christian—there are certain behaviors and thoughts that don't make sense or sit well with a conscience. There are certain things that gnaw at a person's internal compass because God has built this truth into all of us. And the only way we remove its influence is through an ongoing suppression of the truth it reflects.

God tells us clearly that we are without an excuse for not knowing the Source and Author of truth. He has given us plenty of obvious clues. Romans 1:20 says:

For since the creation of the world His invisible attributes, His eternal power and divine nature, have been clearly seen, being understood through what has been made, so that they are without excuse.

God has demonstrated His truth and His presence throughout the matrix of His creation. He has placed in every human heart the knowledge of the reality of His created order. The fact that God knows what He is doing and what He is talking about is evident not only by what He has made, but by what He sustains every moment of every day. It is the fool who has said in his heart that there is no God (Psalm 14:1). That means if a person is an atheist, that person is a fool. A person has to have lost their mind, or at a minimum their conscience, to assume that nobody plus nothing made everything. That is a fairy tale for adults because it is simply not possible. Only when the conscience becomes dull can such blind faith be placed in something as demonstrably wrong as the earth being formed without a God, or Creator, to form it.

But recognizing there is a God who made everything means we should also recognize there is a God who knows how things should operate within the world He has made. We live in a day when that reality has been suppressed so that humanity believes it can conveniently get rid of God. Because if people can get rid of God, they can get rid of guilt. And if they can get rid of guilt, then they can do, be, say, or think whatever they want to. The net result is that chaos replaces character.

As long as God is part of the equation then there is a standard. There is a standard for what is right and what is wrong. There is a standard for how we are to treat each other as human beings made in His image. There exists a standard for how we are to respond to God as our Lord and King over all. And yet, while creation attests to God's power, attributes, and presence (Psalm 19:1), so many people have chosen to intentionally disregard Him.

> **Recognizing there is a God who made everything means we should also recognize there is a God who knows how things should operate within the world He has made.**

So many have chosen to pretend He isn't there simply because we cannot see Him in this realm.

But you and I cannot see air, either, yet we depend upon it for our existence. We can't see wind, but we can see its effects. We can't see oxygen, and yet we still breathe. If we were to declare that air, wind, and oxygen no longer exist because we cannot see them, and we have the right to breathe whatever we want instead, we wouldn't last much longer than to the end of this page or chapter.

You and I can't replace oxygen with whatever we want and still expect to breathe. Neither can we try to replace God and have anything good come of it. Yet that is exactly what our culture is seeking to do.

Paul tells us how a culture seeks to replace God when he continues writing in Romans 1:21–23.

> For even though they knew God, they did not honor Him as God or give thanks, but they became futile in their speculations, and their foolish heart was darkened. Professing to be wise, they became fools, and exchanged the glory of the incorruptible God for an image in the form of corruptible man and of birds and four-footed animals and crawling creatures.

Paul reminds us in this passage that it is futile to seek to replace God. Humanity becomes mired in speculations. We drift backward. Claiming to have wisdom, we turn into fools. When truth is suppressed and God is marginalized, things get dark—very dark. A cursory glance at the chaos in our culture today will clearly show us how dark things have gotten.

This is exactly what Scripture said would happen, so we shouldn't be surprised at the darkness in our land. Proverbs 11:11 tells us of the destruction a city faces when wickedness prevails: "By the mouth of the wicked it is torn down." Cities, cultures, and countries rise through the power of righteousness, not lies. Similarly, wickedness ushers in their destruction.

Proverbs 14:34 puts it like this: "Righteousness exalts a nation, but sin is a disgrace to any people." The political pundits and talk-show hosts debate, argue, blame, and look for fault in every nook and cranny of our culture, but the truth of God's Word makes where the fault lies perfectly clear. Sin and wickedness have been allowed to reign supreme. And God doesn't take well to anyone or anything trying to reign in His rightful place.

Wickedness is what has brought disgrace on our land and disaster within our halls. Righteousness exalts a nation, the writer of Proverbs reminds us, but the mouth of the wicked tears it down. And, by the look of things, we have a lot of people running their mouths right now, seeking to create their own religion, their own idols, and their own rules. We have the idols of notoriety, materialism, racial identity, culture, politics—you name it; there is an idol for anything and everything.

When people do not want to give God the recognition His name demands, they wind up paying the price. You can't have a cafeteria-style God where you get to pick and choose the things you want. You don't get to have God "your way," as if He is your Burger King deity. God defines who He is, and it is we who are to adjust to Him. It's not the other way around.

THREE KINDS OF WRATH

Many people don't realize that God's wrath comes in different forms. Oftentimes when the wrath of God is mentioned, people envision fire and brimstone falling onto a town like Sodom or Gomorrah. And while that can reflect the wrath of God, that is not the primary way God allows His wrath to be revealed today.

When we read earlier that "the wrath of God is revealed," that is referring to a wrath that is taking place presently. It is not talking about the wrath of God in hell. Or the wrath of God to come through some form of judgment. When the wrath of God is "revealed," it means it is present in our world right now. In fact, if you look around you, you will see the wrath of God on display in the lives of many people, and especially in our culture at large.

I call this the *passive* wrath of God. That's one way of distinguishing it from what I referenced earlier with Sodom and Gomorrah—the *active* wrath of God. The flood would be another example of the active wrath of God. When God directly poured the waters onto the earth in order to swallow up its inhabitants, He carried out His active wrath. Most of the wrath of God displayed in the Old Testament reflects this active retribution of God for the evils of sin.

Yet when Jesus died on the cross and was raised again, He realigned God's relationship to the world. Because of the death of Christ, the world was reconciled to God. A shift took place at the cross. So now when God expresses His wrath onto humanity for our sins, it is done differently. We don't see heaven opening up to have fire and brimstone raining down from above. Rather, we experience God's passive wrath displayed in one of three ways.

First, God's wrath takes place when He gives you over to your own ways. We read this in several of the verses in Romans 1:24–28 (emphasis added):

- "Therefore **God gave them over** in the lusts of their hearts to impurity" (v. 24).
- "For this reason **God gave them over** to degrading passions" (v. 26).
- "And just as they did not see fit to acknowledge God any longer, **God gave them over** to a depraved mind, to do those things which are not proper" (v. 28).

You can see the repeated phrase "God gave them over," indicating one of the ways God reveals His passive wrath in lives today. He simply turns humanity over to the impure and unnatural lusts of the flesh. He releases a person to life without Him. He lets you go your own way, freeing you from His influence, restraint, and control.

In essence, God says that if you do not want Him and His truth guiding you, then you can see what life is like without Him. That is the passive wrath of God. My appointment book and cell phone call history are full of people whose souls and spirits, and even their bodies, have been scarred so deeply by living in this form of the passive wrath of God. They have chosen their own way, only to discover that it is a way of death, destruction, emptiness, and pain. I spend a significant amount of my counseling time addressing the issues caused in people when God "gave them over" to themselves so that their degraded desires ruled them.

When your immoral desires tell you what you are going to do and not the other way around, we often call that an *addiction*— when your desires begin to boss you around. Now, an addiction usually starts off as a desire you can still control. But once the passive wrath of God sets in because the person has chosen to live as a suppressor of God's truth, the desire then becomes the one with the whip making all of the decisions. Why? Because once the truth is suppressed, the desire reigns supreme, and our character becomes compromised.

The second way God allows His wrath to be revealed is by allowing the unnatural (that which goes against the created order of things) to be the driving force. As verses 26–27 outline it,

> For this reason God gave them over to degrading passions; for their women exchanged the natural function for that which is unnatural, and in the same way also the men abandoned the natural function of the woman and burned in their desire toward one another, men with men committing indecent acts and receiving in their own persons the due penalty of their error.

As you see in this passage, God gave them over to degrading passions that were unnatural. They were not born with these degrading passions. Their biological framework didn't push them toward these degrading passions. Instead, it was the passive wrath of God that turned them over to crave that which is unnatural.

The Foundation of Biblical Character

There are a lot of sins a person can commit, but God specifically calls out these sins that go against the natural order of things—against the way He created us to live—with regard to His passive wrath. And while we should always show love and compassion to those who are struggling with unnatural sins, we must also realize that these sins are a result of a suppression of the truth—the suppression of God's Word in our world, in our culture, and in our own lives.

That's why we must remember that if we are ever going to address an unnatural situation in a way that brings healing to those involved, we must start with the truth. The problem today is that we don't want to start with the truth that God calls these degrading sins unnatural. Rather, we want to make people comfortable with a lie. So we dance around it. We watch what we say or look the other way. We condone. But no amount of ignoring the truth is going to set people free from the bondage of lies. We are called to speak the truth in love. We are not called to support a lie in love. It is not love to enable someone to continue down the path of destruction.

> No amount of ignoring the truth is going to set people free from the bondage of lies. We are called to speak the truth in love. We are not called to support a lie in love.

While the first two revelations of God's wrath are difficult to experience or witness, the third one is the worst. The first involves deceptive desires ruling over you. The second includes turning you over to degrading passions. But the third one is when God gives you over to a depraved mind. Keep in mind that once you lose your mind, you have lost who you really are. You have lost any ability to manage yourself or to pursue what you truly were made to live out. We read about this third kind of passive wrath in verses 28–32:

And just as they did not see fit to acknowledge God any longer, God gave them over to a depraved mind, to do those things which are not proper, being filled with all unrighteousness, wickedness, greed, evil; full of envy, murder, strife, deceit, malice; they are gossips, slanderers, haters of God, insolent, arrogant, boastful, inventors of evil, disobedient to parents, without understanding, untrustworthy, unloving, unmerciful; and although they know the ordinance of God, that those who practice such things are worthy of death, they not only do the same, but also give hearty approval to those who practice them.

The bottom line of this lengthy passage is that once a person reaches this third and final level of God's passive wrath, they have lost their mind. Once evil is not only practiced but also approved, endorsed, and embraced—and laws are applauded that promote it—the mind is gone. This is why I suggest that America has lost its mind as a nation. We have gone astray from God's truth to such a degree that we not only legalize sin but we also encourage it and seek to cancel anyone who speaks out against it. We have reached the bottom rung of God's revealed wrath.

One of the problems when you read a chapter like this or study a Bible passage like this is that it might make you squirm. It might make you question whether the issues you are facing in your life right now are part of God's revealed passive wrath. It might cause you to wonder if you are a recipient of God's passive wrath or a participant in it, and if you are a participant at this stage in sin's progression, you may wonder how you can get out of it.

Or you might not be thinking about yourself. Maybe you feel that you know God's truth, respect it, and are aligned under His rule as much as you can be—quickly repenting and returning when you drift away. But you might be thinking of a loved one right now. And you are wondering if it's this kind of wrath they are stuck in. You might be wondering if they are trapped by it; they have wandered far from the truth, but you don't know how to help them.

If it's not you or a loved one you are thinking about, it would be hard to read about these spiritual truths and not think of our culture at large. Our culture has turned so far that bent is the new straight. Is there a corrective for this chaos?

Psalm 81 answers this question. This psalm gives hope even if you or someone you love is currently living in the quagmire of God's passive wrath. Consistently bad character and chaotic lives testify to this reality. There is redemption even if you find yourself in a place that feels like divine abandonment. We first review what ushers in God's wrath in this passage, but then we also get to see what we can do to reverse it.

> "But My people did not listen to My voice,
> and Israel did not obey Me.
> So I gave them over to the stubbornness of their heart,
> to walk in their own devices.
> Oh that My people would listen to Me,
> that Israel would walk in My ways!
> I would quickly subdue their enemies
> and turn My hand against their adversaries.
> Those who hate the LORD would pretend obedience to Him,
> and their time of punishment would be forever.
> But I would feed you with the finest of the wheat,
> and with honey from the rock I would satisfy you."
>
> vv. 11–16

It's pretty simple and very straightforward. God makes it clear what we are to do when we find ourselves as recipients of His wrath. He tells us that if we will return to the truth and listen to Him rather than to the world, culture, politicians, our friends, or anyone else—and let Him be our guiding force behind all we do—we will experience a reprieve. We will find release from the wrath. We will find reprieve and release because we will find Him. He will be ready not only to deliver us, but also to defeat our enemies. He will satisfy us with the finest of the fine things to enjoy.

And when God satisfies you, He satisfies you in a way that lasts. He gives peace. Contentment. Fulfillment. Calm. Joy. If you are missing any of these things in your life, I want to remind you how to get them. All you've got to do is return to the God of truth.

4

REDISCOVERING TRUTH

Some of you remember a television show that aired a number of years ago called *Early Edition*. The show followed the life of a man who got tomorrow's newspaper today. And since he knew what was going to happen, he was able to make decisions to adjust that trajectory. His insider information enabled him to prevent accidents and fires and to save lives.

When it comes to the truth, you and I have been given insider information. We have been given the details and the data we need in order to make choices that will produce the best outcomes, namely, stronger character and far less chaos. God has given His family— you and me—the scoop. He has given us the truth.

As a reminder, truth is an absolute standard by which reality is measured. Truth is God's view on any subject matter. Truth lives outside of you. In other words, if it's true then it doesn't matter whether you agree with it. It doesn't matter if you feel it or don't. If it's truth, it is, because God says so. There's no such thing as "my truth" and "your truth." Rather, we have "my belief" or "my perspec- tive" and "your belief" or "your perspective." But when it comes to what is true, that has already been decided by God himself.

The greatest challenge of our lives, and of our world, is the need to adjust ourselves to God's point of view on all subject matters.

When we align under His truth, we reap the benefits and blessings of His rule. When we are not aligned, we walk into the consequences of unwise decisions.

In John 17:17 Jesus prays to the Father about the importance of truth. He says, "Sanctify them in the truth; Your word is truth." Sanctifying someone involves transforming them. The Word of God is a transformative agent in our lives.

At another time, Jesus explained the essential nature of God's truth like this:

> But He answered and said, "It is written, 'MAN SHALL NOT LIVE ON BREAD ALONE, BUT ON EVERY WORD THAT PROCEEDS OUT OF THE MOUTH OF GOD.'"
>
> Matthew 4:4

We do not merely live on the physical food we consume but also on every word that proceeds out of the mouth of God. It is God and His words that hold our world together. He causes the sun to shine, the tides to move, and the food to grow. Without the consistency of His truth, we would not last. Similarly, without the wisdom of His truth, many of the decisions we make lead to dead-end paths.

We live in a day when people in general, and even believers in Christ, are being duped by errant information. Society as a whole is being deceived by lies and partial truths. Whether these lies are personal or are systemic in order to promote ideologies, philosophies, or agendas, they are errant in their presuppositions and directions. They are landmines causing lives to be buried under the debris of lies from the enemy.

We are starving for the truth in today's culture. We read in Amos 8:11–12 about a similar time that came about as a result of God's wrath.

> "Behold, days are coming," declares the Lord GOD,
> "When I will send a famine on the land,

Not a famine for bread or a thirst for water,
But rather for hearing the words of the LORD.
"People will stagger from sea to sea
And from the north even to the east;
They will go to and fro to seek the word of the LORD,
But they will not find it."

As someone staggers when they lack food or water, our culture staggers today due to a lack of truth. In fact, we are staggering on every possible subject matter. We stagger in our relationships. We stagger in our politics and policies. We stagger in our commitments. We stagger in our work. We stagger in what we choose to distract us so that we can simply pass the time.

When there is a famine of God's Word, the people will stagger. Opinions do not carry the stabilizing nutrients nor the sustaining power that truth does. Scripture is the anchor. It is not merely words about God. It is the voice of God in print.

Reading Scripture is like having God here talking with you right now. It is His voice, His wisdom, His perspective—written down. Yet until you decide that you are going to treat it that way, as the resource for absolute truth, then Scripture will simply be one of the many ideas that come across your path. You will glance at it. Read it. Listen to someone espouse it, all the while being unaffected by it.

It remains absolutely critical that you, I, and our culture live according to the right view of Scripture and that we do not fall into the cultural trap of treating it like the queen of England. Queen Elizabeth gets a lot of respect. In fact, when she is not in residence at one of the royal palaces, they fly a different flag until she returns. When her entourage is traveling down the street with her, everyone else pulls over until they pass. The queen gets her props. But just so you know, even though she gets a tremendous amount of respect, she has no real governmental power. She can make no formal governmental decisions. She passes no policies. She doesn't even openly weigh in on political matters. She exists as a figurehead.

Far too many people treat the Bible like the queen of England. They give it some props. They post about it on social media. They let others know that they appreciate it. But they do not give it any power because it does not have the final say. It does not affect their decisions, emotions, or direction.

Until you and I, and our culture as a whole, develop the right and radical understanding of Scripture's authority in our lives, it will be of little use to us. Scripture is the revelation of God. Scripture is divine disclosure. It's similar to sitting in a theater and having someone pull back the curtain so you can see what's behind it. It's the whole scoop. The whole story. It is God giving you and me the content He wants us to have in order to guide us and show us the best way forward. This is spoken of in Isaiah 55, where we read,

> "For My thoughts are not your thoughts,
> Nor are your ways My ways," declares the LORD.
> "For as the heavens are higher than the earth,
> So are My ways higher than your ways
> And My thoughts than your thoughts.
> "For as the rain and the snow come down from heaven,
> And do not return there without watering the earth
> And making it bear and sprout,
> And furnishing seed to the sower and bread to the eater;
> So will My word be which goes forth from My mouth;
> It will not return to Me empty,
> Without accomplishing what I desire,
> And without succeeding in the matter for which I sent it."

vv. 8–11

God tells us in this passage that the reason we need to pay attention to Him and His Word is because He does not think as we do. His thoughts are not our thoughts. He doesn't roll like we do. His ways are not our ways. In fact, they are not even close. As high as the heaven stretches above the earth is how different we are from God. We are finite. We think of things from a limited perspective. God is infinite. He knows all.

Any time you or I try to figure something out independently of God, we have started down the pathway of confusion. God operates and functions on a whole other level.

The words that proceed out of God's mouth are not empty speech. He speaks purposefully. He gives us the divine disclosure. It's as if you were stuck in a maze or an escape room and you called to one of the employees for help—they would give you a clue. They would give you information that you could not have known on your own. The reason they can give it is because they know the way out. They know the path you need to take to reach your destination.

God has disclosed in Scripture all you need to know to reach your divine destination. He has revealed the truth. In theology, we refer to the Word of God as His *revelation*. Revelation is the content, while *inspiration* is the recording of the content, and *illumination* is the Holy Spirit taking the content and applying it directly to you.

WHY WE CAN TRUST GOD'S WORD

Peter describes how we came to have God's Word in 2 Peter 1:

So we have the prophetic word made more sure, to which you do well to pay attention as to a lamp shining in a dark place, until the day dawns and the morning star arises in your hearts. But know this first of all, that no prophecy of Scripture is a matter of one's own interpretation, for no prophecy was ever made by an act of human will, but men moved by the Holy Spirit spoke from God.

vv. 19–21

Revelation (what God wanted to say) came through inspiration, the Holy Spirit moving in the minds of the Old and New Testament authors of Scripture to write what God wanted written. The Holy Spirit oversaw what was being written and that which would make up what we refer to as the *canon* of Scripture.

Thus, what we have in the Bible is what God wanted to be in the Bible. He tells us that nothing in His Word came about through sheer human will. It came about because God oversaw that which was in the mind, which then flowed to the hand and was written down. It was all overseen by Him.

The Greek word used for our translation of *moved* in this passage has the imagery attached to it of a sail on a sailboat being blown by the wind. It is the wind that determines where the sailboat goes. It's also a picture of a leaf being blown in the wind. It's the wind that determines where the leaf goes. The Holy Spirit breathed His breath into each and every writer of Scripture in order to guide and direct what was written. The result of this is men using their own personalities and perspectives coupled with the Holy Spirit's leading to create Scripture.

And while men had a part to play in the compiling of Scripture, the imperfection of humanity did not stain it. In the same way that God protected Jesus (the Living Word) from the sin nature of His mother, He protected the written Word from the sin natures of its authors. That's how we can have a perfect Savior and a perfect Scripture, because the perfect Holy Spirit blocked anything errant or sinful from entering into the equation.

And if you look at Scripture from a historical vantage point, it will also stand the test of scrutiny. Scripture is not just a divinely authorized message from God. It's also a history book. The only way you and I know anything in history that we weren't around to witness ourselves is through historical records. We know about George Washington even though we never talked to him, met him, or heard him speak because we have a historical record that reveals him to us. We have documents to declare who he was.

Have you ever heard anyone state that George Washington or Abraham Lincoln didn't exist simply because they have never seen them? There is a consensus as to their existence due to the historical witnesses and recordings of their lives. Similarly, when you and I examine the historical record of Scripture, it passes the test of accuracy as well. There were sixty-six books written over 1,500 years by just over forty authors, and the historical accuracy within that span of time confirms itself. For example, in Micah 5:2 there is a written record that the Savior would be born in the small town of Bethlehem. Centuries later, this is where Jesus was born.

In fact, when people were debating whether the earth was flat, Isaiah had already written that the earth was round. When people discovered oil in the Middle East, the record of Scripture had already stated that when Noah built the ark, he built it with pitch and tar. Wherever you have pitch and tar, you have oil. The record speaks for itself. Whether it has to do with science, geography, anthropology, or prophecy, the Bible has been proven to be accurate on all of these things. The few times someone thought they found a discrepancy or inaccuracy in Scripture over the years, they found out a few years later that *they* were wrong—not Scripture. Over and over again, the Bible has been authenticated as a historical document, an accurate record of time, people, and events. It is a self-authenticating document and more than sufficient to shape or rebuild your character and reverse the chaos in your life.

Jesus declared that even heaven and earth would pass away before the smallest detail in the Word of God would go unfulfilled. We read Jesus' words in Matthew 5:18, "For truly I say to you, until heaven and earth pass away, not the smallest letter or stroke shall pass from the Law until all is accomplished." The "letter or stroke" Jesus refers to are the smallest markings in the Hebrew alphabet. He tells us that Scripture is so complete, comprehensive, and true that the tiniest strokes of it will be fulfilled—every last detail.

In fact, God warns us in Revelation 22:18–19 that anyone who adds to Scripture will bring plagues upon themselves, and whoever takes away from Scripture God will take away his part from the Tree of Life. It is God who is protecting and preserving His Word. Time and time again we see this stated:

- ▸ "I testify to everyone who hears the words of the prophecy of this book: if anyone adds to them, God will add to him the plagues which are written in this book" (Revelation 22:18).
- ▸ "Heaven and earth will pass away, but My words will not pass away" (Matthew 24:35).
- ▸ "Every word of God is tested; He is a shield to those who take refuge in Him. Do not add to His words or He will reprove you, and you will be proved a liar" (Proverbs 30:5–6).
- ▸ "The words of the LORD are pure words; as silver tried in a furnace on the earth, refined seven times" (Psalm 12:6).

God's Word is pure, undefiled truth. Yet you and I live in a post-truth world. We live in a world that prefers deception facilitated by evil. In fact, many Christians prefer deception facilitated by evil because it makes them feel good.

But until we discover our need to turn to the truth of God's Word instead of to the lies of the world, we will never solve the cultural, racial, relational, political, or myriad other problems plaguing our nation today. Until we discover what it means to truly abide in and align under the truth of God's Word, we will continue to experience the chaos and confusion that engulf us.

Jesus told us clearly in John 8:31 that those who abide in the truth of His words are truly His disciples. If you flip that, it makes it clear that when you do not abide in Christ's Word and align under the truth, you are not a kingdom disciple. *To abide* means "to hang out, stay, or remain in." For example, you abide in your home. You live there. To abide in the truth of Christ, you need to live with His perspective. You need to live according to His world view, with a desire to know what Jesus feels, thinks, and says about any subject you are dealing with.

You cannot be His disciple and ignore His Word. You cannot be His disciple and reject His Word. You cannot say you are a kingdom disciple and not hold God's inerrant Word in the highest esteem.

What's missing in our culture today is Christians who will stand on God's Word with the right attitude and right spirit of kindness and humility, but also with crystal-clear clarity as to what it says because His Word is flawless. His Word makes no mistakes about anything it addresses, and it addresses everything we need to know. Yet in our post-Christian environment, respect for God's Word may be the most you get. Not yielding to it. Not aligning under it or being governed by it. And this is why we are living in chaos.

> You cannot be His disciple and ignore His Word. You cannot be His disciple and reject His Word. You cannot say you are a kingdom disciple and not hold God's inerrant Word in the highest esteem.

America has a Constitution, and the Supreme Court's role is to uphold the Constitution through application of the law consistent with the Constitution. The Constitution is the superintending document to which legislation and executive action must conform. So while one group might disagree with what another group says or desires, and their disagreement can lead to protests, fighting, and fussing, neither group has the final say-so. The Supreme Court is the last avenue of appeal and the final authority, based on its interpretation of the Constitution.

Jesus tells us in John 10:35 that the Scripture is our final say-so. He says, "If he called them gods, to whom the word of God came (and the Scripture cannot be broken)."

When it says that "the Scripture cannot be broken," it means that it can't be canceled. You cannot serve cancel culture notice to God's Word. *To break* in this case means "to annul, cancel, or render it inoperative." Sure, people can try to cancel Scripture, but it will not be canceled. We will be canceled first.

In fact, the world and our culture try to cancel God's Word all of the time, only to find out that the repercussions blow back on them harshly. You've seen it as much as I have. The culture is desperately trying to cancel genders. To cancel morality. To cancel families. And to cancel hope. Whatever the particular object, they are seeking to cancel the truth because people are much more easily manipulated toward the evil agendas of the enemy when they are confused, uncertain, and distant from God.

But Jesus stated plainly that the Scripture cannot be broken. Truth cannot be canceled. The Bible cannot be amended, annulled, or tweaked to fit an agenda outside of God's kingdom purposes for which it was originally established. There are times when it may look like the truth is losing the battle, but it always comes back to demonstrate its ultimate authority.

Keep in mind, people don't reject the Bible because it contradicts itself. They reject the Bible because it contradicts them. They don't want to be contradicted or corrected. That's why men suppress the truth (see Romans 1:18). Humanity suppresses the truth because people don't want the truth telling them what to do. They don't want the truth influencing or controlling their decision-making. Second Timothy 3 summarizes it this way:

> But evil men and impostors will proceed from bad to worse, deceiving and being deceived. You, however, continue in the things you have learned and become convinced of, knowing from whom you have learned them, and that from childhood you have known the sacred writings which are able to give you the wisdom that leads to salvation through faith which is in Christ Jesus. All Scripture is inspired by God and profitable for teaching, for reproof, for correction, for training in righteousness; so that the man of God may be adequate, equipped for every good work.

vv. 13–17

Scripture exists to teach, reprove, correct, and train us. We are to be different because of our interaction with the truth of God's Word. Yet because people often want to make their own decisions and go their own way, they set God's Word to the side or put it on the mantel as another piece of decor in their home. But that is not what God intended His Word to be. From the first verse in Genesis to the last verse in Revelation, Scripture is God-breathed (*theopneustos*) with the intention of guiding, correcting, and teaching. When allowed to do its job, Scripture transforms our character.

When you and I learn that we must treat God's Word as it was created to be treated, not just as something to make us feel good when we choose a passage to read, that is when it will become profitable in our lives and in our land.

An airplane needs a control tower to direct the pilot to the final destination as well as to keep the pilot and passengers from harm along the way. Similarly, a life on earth needs a control tower. There are many times this world gets cloudy, stormy, and dangerous. There are many times when you cannot see the place where you are headed or the disastrous paths around you. But if you will look to God's Word for teaching, correction, and direction, you will know how to navigate the challenges and chaos of this world. The Bible is our control tower. It is our source of all truth.

A man one day went to visit a doctor because he wasn't feeling well. The doctor performed an examination and then prescribed some medication for him. The doctor even had the nurse call in the prescription to the local pharmacy, where the man went and picked it up. A week later, the man called the doctor and complained that he was still sick. The doctor asked how much of the medication he had taken. "I haven't taken any," the man replied. "I haven't opened it."

The doctor responded, "Well, that's your problem. Take it. And don't call me again until you do."

See, a lot of us will pick up the Bible and carry it under our arm. Or put it on the side table or by our bed. But we will fail to open it to see what is inside. We won't open it to read, discern, learn, and be impacted by its truth. When we fail to treat Scripture as the absolute inerrant, authoritative voice of God in print, it is we who will pay the price. We will pay the price in our lives, relationships, work, finances, peace of mind, and so much more. The things that plague us will only increase when we neglect to learn and apply God's truth to the situations and challenges we face.

The other day I was in my car, and the side mirror had collapsed. I couldn't get it to open up to where it was supposed to be. So I decided to figure it out. I fiddled with that mirror, pushed it, pulled it, and sought to maneuver that mirror for close to twenty minutes. I knew I couldn't drive without a mirror to show me the cars behind and beside me, so I stayed with the task, seeking a solution.

Eventually, it dawned on me that in the glove box of my car was an owner's manual. Now, honestly speaking, I hadn't opened that book before, even though I owned it. I hadn't read it, even though it was close by me every time I drove. But I had become so satisfied with the basics of operation that I never explored the book.

Until I was stuck. Until I couldn't go anywhere and needed that book. So this time, I grabbed it. It didn't take me too long to figure out how to fix my mirror once I decided to use the book that was designed exactly for that purpose—to help me drive my car.

It wasn't until something wasn't working for me and I couldn't figure it out that I remembered the manufacturer of my car had provided a manual for me. In hindsight, I wasted time and experienced a lot of frustration because I put off going to the place that held the answer to my problem.

Likewise, many believers today are wasting time and experiencing a lot of frustration because they refuse to go to the one place that holds the answers to any problems they face. If we as the body of Christ would simply return to the Word of God as our source of truth and then do what it says, we could solve the issues creating the chaos around us and within us.

You are I are to be people of the truth. In order to be people of the truth, we must be people of the Word. We must be people of Scripture. We must make God's Word our guide for our thoughts, words, and actions. When we do that, we will discover the powerfully transformative impact His Word will have on our lives, our surroundings, and our nation.

5

RETURNING TO THE TRUTH

A ninety-five-year-old man was talking to his doctor one day. He said, "Doc, I just want you to know that my wife is pregnant." He had married a woman a whole lot younger than he and was feeling pretty significant now that she was pregnant.

The doctor paused a little while when he heard the news. Then he smiled and said, "There once was a man who was absent-minded. He went on a safari and came across a lion. But instead of pulling out his gun to shoot the lion, he pulled out his golf club and shot the lion with the club, and he killed it!"

The patient looked at the doctor and said, "Doc, that's impossible! Somebody else must have done that!"

The doctor just smiled again and replied, "Exactly."

It's easy to think you are more than you really are. As this older man did, it's easy for us to have the wrong view of our abilities. When it comes to human understanding, we're not "all that and a bag of chips." We exist as finite creatures.

Most of us have lived long enough to learn that things we once believed to be true and acted on as if they were true sometimes turn out to be a deception. We all know what it is to have abandoned truth, fallen for a lie, and paid the consequences for it. In fact, we're watching our world do that before our very eyes.

In order for the truth to work in us and in our lives, it must be received. It must be believed. We must allow humility to enter our hearts in such a way that we understand God is the Author of truth, and we are not. That's why 1 Thessalonians 2:13 reads,

> For this reason we also constantly thank God that when you received the word of God which you heard from us, you accepted it not as the word of men, but for what it really is, the word of God, which also performs its work in you who believe.

For the Word of Truth to work in building kingdom virtue in our lives—for it to do what it was designed and revealed to accomplish—it must be received. You must welcome it in. When you don't do that, however, it doesn't change the truth from being the truth. It just changes the power of the truth in working for you.

When we talk about receiving it, keep in mind that it's the truth of God you need to receive. That doesn't necessarily mean what a preacher or even a biblical scholar said, or what was printed in a Christian magazine. Many people peddle the Word out of a wrong motivation or are simply misguided themselves even though their motives might be pure. Paul warned us of this in 2 Timothy 4:1–5, which reads,

> I solemnly charge you in the presence of God and of Christ Jesus, who is to judge the living and the dead, and by His appearing and His kingdom: preach the word; be ready in season and out of season; reprove, rebuke, exhort, with great patience and instruction. For the time will come when they will not endure sound doctrine; but wanting to have their ears tickled, they will accumulate for themselves teachers in accordance to their own desires, and will turn away their ears from the truth and will turn aside to myths. But you, be sober in all things, endure hardship, do the work of an evangelist, fulfill your ministry.

Paul urged Timothy to stick with the truth. Just as in our day, there were people then seeking to say what "itching ears" wanted to hear. Good-sounding popular myths fill pulpits all across our nation because so many people have abandoned the truth. Far too many people want to be placated. They want to be made to feel good. They want a doughnut sermon—one that satisfies the taste buds but has no nutritional value.

Too many people want doughnut Christianity—a religion that makes them feel good but is void of truth. Sadly, they don't mind the absence of truth because they like how it sounds and how it feels.

One way you can tell when a preacher has failed biblically is if all of his sermons merely make people feel good. Paul told Timothy to use the truth in order to rebuke, to reprove, and even to correct errant thinking and behavior. Paul didn't encourage Timothy to preach on politics, theories, or prosperity. He told him to preach the Word, in season and out. He was to preach it when it was easy, and when it was not.

Similarly, preachers today are to preach the Word when their audience nods in agreement, and when they don't. When they clap, and when they boo. When it affirms, and when it offends. Because, like it or not, the truth is going to offend someone somewhere at some time. But it's a necessary offense if it shows the way for that person to go, to adjust or realign themselves under God, and to build within them kingdom virtues.

As a pastor, I know this is not always easy. I know the pressure is there to please. Or to quit when the burden of preaching the truth becomes too much. But still, we are to preach the Word.

In the church where I pastor, we have a stained-glass mural on the wall behind the pulpit, above the baptismal. Across the bottom of the beautiful mural is written *Preach the Word*. Those words are there because my wife, Lois, asked that they be added many years ago, shortly before the mural was created. I wasn't surprised by her request because it reflected her heart and her love for God's Word.

Many of you reading this book know that I lost my wife to cancer on December 30, 2019. What you may not know is that I was scheduled to preach the very next day at our New Year's Eve service. And as I was sitting there at home deciding whether I could or would preach, assessing whether I even had the strength to do so—because no one would have blamed me for staying home at that time—I remembered her saying, "Preach the Word." I remembered Lois's urging to each of us when she was diagnosed the second time with cancer that none of us in the family were to pull back from ministry. She urged us to keep pursuing and carrying out what God had called us to do.

It wasn't convenient for me to go and preach that night, just one day after my wife of nearly fifty years had gone on to Glory. In fact, it was the most inconvenient time of my life. I would have preferred to stay home with the curtains shut. But God had called me to "preach the Word." And that meant when it was convenient and when it wasn't. So that's what I did. Because the church is to be that place on earth where those committed to the truth live out that truth. We might live it out imperfectly at times, but the church is to be the place where we at least try.

THE CHURCH AND THE TRUTH

Communities are filled with grocery stores. They are repositories of food. We take advantage of grocery stores because what they offer is essential for our physical well-being. Grocery stores are not ancillary to a community's ability to thrive. They allow for individuals to get what they need to be nutritionally satisfied.

Now, what would be dissatisfactory in a community is a grocery store that sold rotten food. Despite the fact that this store would advertise fresh food and identify itself as a repository of fresh food, anyone shopping there would find only rotten food. In that situation, the store bearing the name of a supplier of wholesome food but not carrying the products to back the name would be a fake.

As we saw in the previous example, a repository is a container, a storehouse of sorts. A repository for medicine is called a pharmacy. If you go to the records building downtown, which is a repository of information about people, locations, and history, you'll find a wealth of insight not available outside of this storehouse.

God also has a repository. He has a storehouse—a community location for your spiritual well-being, life transformation, and development of kingdom virtue. This is a place where you are supposed to go to get good spiritual food—a place to eat well spiritually and relationally. God has scattered throughout every community nearly everywhere in our nation a repository for spiritual nourishment, available to those who live in the vicinity.

God's repository, the church, is to function as a deliverer or dispenser of truth. It is to be a place where people who are seeking to know truth can receive guidance on how to locate and discern truth in God's Word.

The church is the location God has singled out that does not find its first obligation in the culture—or in the racial, cultural, or gender identity of a particular group. The commitment of a church is not first to how people were raised or where they live. The church exists as a repository to supply nutritious spiritual sustenance, as opposed to rotten food, because it is committed to one overarching goal, and that is the declaration of truth. Essentially, the church is God's spiritual grocery store, where people are to go to access the truth.

Paul shares this mentality when he writes to his spiritual son in the ministry, Timothy:

> Although I hope to come to you soon, I am writing you these instructions so that, if I am delayed, you will know how people ought to conduct themselves in God's household, which is the church of the living God, the pillar and foundation of the truth.
>
> 1 Timothy 3:14–15 NIV

69

Timothy lived in a very secular city at the time of this writing. It was a bustling part of Asia Minor called Ephesus. He had helped establish a church there, which we can refer to for our purposes as Ephesus Bible Fellowship. Timothy served as the lead pastor while Paul served as his spiritual mentor.

Paul sought to disciple Timothy throughout this process. One of the main components of his discipleship training was to remind Timothy that God's household exists to serve as the pillar and foundation of truth. Paul urged him to keep this in the forefront of his mind and his motives so that when people came to his church, they would be getting the truth so that proper Christian conduct might be communicated and, as necessary, behaviors corrected.

To give you some background on the town in which Timothy served, it was full of idolatry, materialism, witchcraft, social decay, and errant teaching. It was an influencer's paradise of wrong ideas. So when Paul reminded Timothy to make the church the pillar and foundation of truth, he was urging him to go against the culture. He reminded him to hold fast to the truth despite the ideologies, theories, and perspectives imbuing the minds of its citizens.

In spite of everything being taught in education, in corporations, or through governmental regimes, Timothy needed to keep the church solidly connected to the truth of God for the development of kingdom virtue. Now, this isn't always easy to do, especially when the culture carries so much power in purporting "its truth" as "the truth" and everyone else as "intolerant."

But Paul reminded Timothy why it was so important to keep teaching the truth despite the difficulties. He referenced the cultural chaos and confusion as he wrote to him over and over concerning his role. We read some examples throughout his letter:

> ▶ "As I urged you upon my departure for Macedonia, remain on at Ephesus so that you may instruct certain men not to teach strange doctrines" (1 Timothy 1:3).

- "But the Spirit explicitly says that in later times some will fall away from the faith, paying attention to deceitful spirits and doctrines of demons" (1 Timothy 4:1).
- "Such teachings come through hypocritical liars, whose consciences have been seared as with a hot iron" (1 Timothy 4:2 NIV).

It was this cultural climate that prompted Paul to write that all church leaders must keep hold of "the mystery of the faith with a clear conscience" (1 Timothy 3:9). It actually doesn't sound a whole lot different from our world today.

We're living in a duped society alongside duped neighbors consuming duped media producing a decrepit environment. The church is to be the beacon of truth where people can go to be reminded of what is real and what is deception. The church is not to be a social club, a fraternity, or a sorority. It's called a "family" and a "household."

In 1 Timothy 5:1–2, Paul refers to older men as "fathers," and older women as "mothers." A family is a regularly attached group of people, and in the church's case, those who choose to become equipped with God's point of view.

Scripture knows nothing of an unchurched Christian. There is simply no such thing. A person might say, "Well, I don't have to go to church to be a Christian." And they could be absolutely right. You become a Christian by faith alone in Christ alone. Similarly, you don't have to go home to be married. But stay away long enough and your relationship will be affected.

> **The church is to be the beacon of truth where people can go to be reminded of what is real and what is deception.**

God has established and determined that the church will exist as the environment where people are to connect with each other around the central pillar of His Word, the truth. We are not to live independently as spiritual orphans. Many people need to return to church following the prolonged pandemic lockdown when a lot of churches were closed. Similarly, we also need to return to the truth.

Oftentimes people want the church like a teenager wants a family. Teens want to stay in their room until it's time to eat. They don't care to contribute to the needs of the home. Similarly, when people are about to get married, or they have a problem, they'll call the church. But when it comes to everyday living, they assume they can work that out on their own.

Another way to describe it is that many people treat the church like a membership at the gym. They are members, but they never go! And, if they were honest, they would admit that it shows: The reason why they are spiritually flabby and have no muscle when it comes to life's challenges is because the spiritual workout is not taking place.

Being part of the church includes a commitment to be identified and dynamically involved with a loyal body of believers who are learning to live kingdom lives under the lordship of Jesus Christ. It includes both identity and involvement. It's not about sitting, soaking, and souring. It also includes serving.

When a church functions as God intends it to function, it becomes a powerful force against evil. Jesus said that even Satan's forces will not prevail against the church.

> "I also say to you that you are Peter, and upon this rock I will build My church; and the gates of Hades will not overpower it. I will give you the keys of the kingdom of heaven; and whatever you bind on earth shall have been bound in heaven, and whatever you loose on earth shall have been loosed in heaven."
>
> Matthew 16:18–19

God doesn't skip the church house to fix the White House. He doesn't skip His spiritual grocery store to go to genetically modified and engineered food sources. God has built His church to serve as a pure repository of truth, untainted by the world's viewpoints. Our job as representatives of the King of Kings and the Lord of Lords in the church and outwardly to the world is to inform culture about what heaven thinks on every subject. That's why the Lord's Prayer says, "Thy kingdom come, Thy will be done on earth, as it is in heaven" (KJV). We are to use the "keys of the kingdom" to usher in heaven's rule on earth.

Have you ever been in a hurry and unable to locate your keys? You know that one thing is certain when you can't find your keys: You aren't going anywhere. Or maybe you are like me in that you have so many keys on your keychain that you don't remember what they all go to anymore. They become useless. They can't open anything for you because you don't know what they were created to open.

Similarly, the keys of the kingdom have been given to open doors of God's authority on earth. As we read earlier in Matthew 16, "whatever you loose on earth shall have been loosed in heaven." The keys represent the authority of God being vested in humanity.

The reason why we can be a nation with all of these churches on all of these corners with all of these programs and all of these members led by all of these preachers yet still have all of this mess is because we are using the wrong keys. We are using cultural keys, racial keys, gender keys, ideological keys, or humanistic keys rather than kingdom keys.

The primary test to determine whether the church is being the church Jesus Christ established is that "the gates of Hades" are not prevailing against it. Neither hell (Hades) nor humans acting on hell's agenda will be able to stop the true church of Christ. When the church operates according to the truth of the keys of the kingdom—which means aligning under God's viewpoint on every subject—the church will prevail.

YOU ARE THE CHURCH

Over and over again in the New Testament, we read that Jesus is the head of the church and we are His body to enact and carry forward

His agenda. That's why each of you reading this book should make it your aim to become a kingdom disciple who lives as a kingdom servant making a kingdom impact.

For example, if you are a lawyer, then you are not just a lawyer. You are God's representative in the Bar Association so that the Bar Association sees what God looks like when God tries a case. If you are a doctor, you are God's representative in the medical field so that the medical field sees what God looks like when God helps hurting people. If you are a teacher, you are God's representative in the classroom so that the classroom sees what God looks like when God teaches truth.

You and I are to represent God and His viewpoint in every sphere of life. We are to represent the "living God" as the "pillar and foundation of the truth." When Paul wrote these words to Timothy, both Timothy and the others who attended the church in Ephesus would understand what he meant when he referred to the truth as a "pillar and foundation." This is because in Ephesus was located one of the Seven Wonders of the World at that time. It was a temple known as the Temple of Artemis. People traveled from all over the world to come and see this massive statue and tribute to the goddess of all gods, Artemis (also known as Diana).

> You and I are to represent God and His viewpoint in every sphere of life. We are to represent the living God as the pillar and foundation of the truth.

If you read through Acts 19, you'll see that they had built an entire economy around Artemis. The location was such a popular destination that they had established businesses to support the tourists and visitors who traveled there. It became a place of economic development and entertainment.

The interesting element about the temple itself is that it was surrounded by hundreds of pillars that held up the roof. The temple was so massive that it required an enormous number of pillars on the foundation in order to support the structure.

Thus, when Paul chose to describe truth as "pillars" and the "foundation," he wasn't just using random imagery. He referenced something everyone in Ephesus knew very well in order to make his point. The truth of God's Word is to serve as both the groundwork and the reinforcing structure for all else. It is to build up lives, families, communities, and our entire nation. Without it, the entire structure collapses.

Paul reminds us in this passage that in God's house, we are to operate according to God's rules. Our conduct must be conducive to the truth. That's not too much to ask, after all, since we are in God's house.

If you were to come over to my house, you would need to abide by my rules. For example, if you were used to doing recreational drugs in your house, you would need to leave them behind when you came into mine. Because in my house, we don't make room for recreational drugs. Now, I understand that you may do things differently in your house. But in my house, my rules apply.

God calls all of creation His house. We read about this in Psalm 24:1, "The earth is the LORD's, and all it contains, the world, and those who dwell in it." Since this whole world is God's house, He has a right to ask us to abide by His rules. When we choose not to do so, we—and those around us—pay the price.

Now, if you go out and create your own world, you can make your own rules. But until you make your own world, you need to abide by God's rules in His world. Because when you don't, you place yourself in conflict with the Owner of the house. And we all know that never ends well for the guest.

We are living in a world so embroiled in conflict with God that it now spills out to everyone else, all because we do not want to accept His truth. And while that should not surprise us about the world at large, it ought to shock us about the church.

When a person goes to a hospital, he or she assumes they are going to a repository of health. They go there to be healed. What's more, most of us want the doctor to tell us the truth. We wouldn't want a doctor who says, "Oh, you're fine," when you really aren't and need to be treated. Even if the truth is negative, we want the truth from our doctors and healthcare workers because that is how we can begin to be helped. Whether that help comes through medicine, surgery, or a treatment regimen, the only way you'll get it is if the doctor tells the truth.

But far too many people in the church today are not being told the truth. They are being told, "Oh, you're fine," or, "Oh, that behavior is fine," when it's not. The church is supposed to be a hospital, not a hospice. People don't go to church to be comfortable as they are dying. They come to church to heal their heart, soul, and life as well as to discover peace, joy, and contentment.

Yet we are faced with a pandemic of pastors telling people stuff that will never help them live but just makes them feel good as they die. Whether that death is relational, spiritual, emotional, or the like, death results when truth is denied.

The body of Christ has built our collective life around appetizers while skipping the main meal. As long as there is fun, laughter, music, and food trucks, we're fine. But start speaking the truth, and people get uncomfortable. People pull back. They stop attending. It's very evident that not everyone wants to hear the truth. But until we become more willing to both speak the truth with love and hear the truth that is being spoken to us, we will continue in the loop of chaos we are in right now. The only way out of the loop is to learn to embrace this core foundation of values known as the truth, as well as to practice sharing it with others in a way that glorifies God and enables them to receive it. Let's take a look at how that is done in the next chapter.

6

MERGING LOVE
WITH TRUTH

When a football player kicks a field goal, it has to go through the uprights to be considered good. If you are unfamiliar with football, the uprights are the two posts that extend into the air at each end of the field. And if this is the first book of mine you are reading, yes, I do reference football a lot. It's my favorite sport, and it's filled with illustrations. In this example, the ball must pass between the posts if it is to count for points. If the ball goes to the left or to the right side, outside of the posts, it is considered no good and no points are awarded.

Everyone who plays, referees, and watches football are all on the same page when it comes to what these posts signify and how three points are attributed to a team when a ball goes through them. It's called a field goal.

God has two posts when it comes to our maturity in Christ and how to develop kingdom virtue as His followers, especially related to how we communicate with each other. I want us to look at this standard for our speech, particularly in light of how it seems to be tossed by the wayside recently. Whether it's watching people speak to each other on talk shows, in the news, on social media, or in person, honorable speech appears to have gone missing.

I'm alarmed at how accusatory and insulting speech has become when people disagree with each other. This type of speech leaves no room for dialogue, mutual learning, or growth. What it does is shut down the conversation altogether. We used to call the speech we are witnessing now *bullying*. But whether you refer to it as verbal vitriol, language politics, or bullying, that doesn't change the reality that our speech as believers, which is supposed to be modeled on Christ in His Word, appears instead to reflect the common cultural climate. How do we expect to win anyone over to God and His kingdom agenda if our speech sounds no different from the hatred and judgment so prevalent today?

The two posts, or standards, for our speech are given to us in Ephesians 4:14–16, where we read,

> As a result, we are no longer to be children, tossed here and there by waves and carried about by every wind of doctrine, by the trickery of men, by craftiness in deceitful scheming; but speaking the truth in love, we are to grow up in all aspects into Him who is the head, even Christ, from whom the whole body, being fitted and held together by what every joint supplies, according to the proper working of each individual part, causes the growth of the body for the building up of itself in love.

I've included the surrounding verses for context, but the two posts referred to in the passage we just read are (1) speaking the truth and (2) speaking it in love. The two posts for how we are to successfully navigate cultural waters in our communication as Christians are truth and love. Anything outside of those two standards does not count as a kingdom virtue. It misses the mark.

Now, truth refers to the content of what we say while love refers to both the motivation for and the manner of saying it. We are not to defer to one standard over the other because the two posts stand side by side as a determining factor of whether we score in living out kingdom character.

Paul's concern in this passage surrounds the maturity of the Christians to whom he wrote. He wants them to grow up. The reality of his day was that many believers were still immature and carnal. They were being blown about by every wind of doctrine. Unfortunately, it seems, not much has changed.

People seem content to change beliefs about what is true simply because of what the latest social media influencer or newscaster has said, or even what a family member or friend has told them. When the wind blows a certain way and it seems right or feels good, they'll go with that. Then, when it blows another way, or things get shaky in the first direction, they'll change and go with something new. People can change so fast because they haven't matured to the point where God's Word serves as the anchor of all truth.

When you go to a doctor, they often ask you to stick out your tongue. They do this because they are looking for things on or about your tongue that could indicate something wrong deeper inside of you. The Bible declares that a person's speech also reveals whether there is something wrong deeper inside of him or her. What you say, and how you say it, reflects your heart. James 1:26 puts it like this: "If anyone thinks himself to be religious, and yet does not bridle his tongue but deceives his own heart, this man's religion is worthless."

Basically, if you can't control your tongue, your "religion is worthless." Now, I understand that occasionally you and I will make mistakes. But what Paul is referring to here is the ongoing process and revelation of spiritual maturity. If your normal mode of operation is to belittle, judge, gossip, scorn, mock, lie, or engage in any other verbal vice known to mankind, then you might want to reconsider where your relationship with Jesus Christ sits.

You may want to examine where you are today as opposed to where you were several months ago, or a year ago. Has your mouth (what you say, how you say it, and why you choose to say it) fallen more in line, going between the two goal posts of truth and love, or are you still speaking from the flesh? This is how you can know if you are growing in godly character and kingdom virtues.

- ▸ Is your speech improving?
- ▸ Do you feel the need to voice every thought you have, or have you learned to be content to listen to others as well?
- ▸ Do you want to have the last word, or are you willing to let things slide for the sake of love and kindness?
- ▸ Do you speak as if what you say is the end-all-be-all on every topic, or do you leave room open for someone to perhaps know more than you do?
- ▸ Do your words reflect a heart of faith or fear, calm or chaos, peace or pride?

There are many ways to gauge your kingdom virtue, but the primary one is by what you say. Your mouth reveals your heart. Jesus explained it like this,

Peter said to Him, "Explain the parable to us." Jesus said, "Are you still lacking in understanding also? Do you not understand that everything that goes into the mouth passes into the stomach, and is eliminated? But the things that proceed out of the mouth come from the heart, and those defile the man. For out of the heart come evil thoughts, murders, adulteries, fornications, thefts, false witness, slanders. These are the things which defile the man; but to eat with unwashed hands does not defile the man."

Matthew 15:15–20

What you say and how you say it reveals the real you. The kingdom of God ought to reflect God's kingdom virtues. But instead it seems a shift has occurred. We are being inundated with information and communication modeled after Facebook posts, Instagram feeds, Twitter rants, chats, messaging, memes, and more. We've got unhealthy communication going every which way. Not only is it often full of lies, but it is just as frequently full of angst and evil ways of communicating with or about others.

As kingdom followers, we are to be speaking the truth in love. We are to speak according to the absolute standard by which reality is measured—to speak that which reflects God's view on any subject. It doesn't matter how many people agree with you. It doesn't matter how many people like what you have to say. It doesn't even matter how you feel about it. Once God says something is true, it is to dominate the environment and atmosphere of His people because we are seeking to function according to His kingdom world view.

> As kingdom followers, we are to be speaking the truth in love. We are to speak according to the absolute standard by which reality is measured—to speak that which reflects God's view on any subject.

People who have not learned to manage their speech have similarly not learned how to manage other aspects of their lives. The chaos in their heart, mind, and decisions shows up in what they have to say. All manner of speech that is inconsistent with the character of God indicates something is wrong deep inside that person. Whether it is joking that aims to hurt people, gossip, profanity, harsh judgment, sarcasm, insults, vulgarity, disrespect, unkindness, rudeness, or any other, it merely reflects the chaos within the person saying it.

James 3:2 outlines this connection between what a person says and his or her inability to manage other aspects of their life. We read, "For we all stumble in many ways. If anyone does not stumble in what he says, he is a perfect man, able to bridle the whole body as well."

If you want a peek at how a person is doing, just listen to what they say. Because if the speech is a mess, then the rest is a mess too. The tongue is the indicator of a person's internal life.

TRUTH AND THE TAMING OF THE TONGUE

Speech is an indicator of a culture's health as well. A glance around will alert you that we are living in a world of putrid speech and hateful communication. Just scroll through some of the things people are saying about and to one another. Even Christians are getting caught up in this hate-filled way of dismissing and insulting others who have a different viewpoint.

We recently experienced this as a ministry when something was posted by my son, Jonathan, which, when taken out of context, set off a tirade of hate-filled comments and replies to those comments. Before you knew it, entire conversations were being had between social media followers, very few of which reflected a page dedicated to the glory of God.

When I looked at some of the profiles of the people posting, I was alarmed to read in the bios things like "I love Jesus Christ," or "Sharing God's love," or even "Jesus first!" Just from the words, statements, and unfounded accusations being posted as comments, it was clear Jesus was nowhere in the vicinity. When a person gets so caught up in criticizing or insulting someone else, it shows his or her own lack of spiritual maturity. Ephesians 4:29–31 explains what a mature believer's words should sound like:

> Let no unwholesome word proceed from your mouth, but only such a word as is good for edification according to the need of the moment, so that it will give grace to those who hear. Do not grieve the Holy Spirit of God, by whom you were sealed for the day of redemption. Let all bitterness and wrath and anger and clamor and slander be put away from you, along with all malice.

Paul reminds us in this passage that what we say can literally "grieve the Holy Spirit of God." You make the Holy Spirit sad when you use or post "unwholesome words." Unwholesome words are those that are designed to hurt and destroy, not to heal and help. As believers we are to speak the truth in love. That is to be our orientation. Proverbs 10:11 says, "The mouth of the righteous is a fountain of life, but the mouth of the wicked conceals violence." Words matter. They either produce life or they create chaos.

First Thessalonians 5:11 tells us that our communication should bring help to people, not harm: "Therefore encourage one another and build up one another, just as you also are doing." We should never use our words to tear people down. Thus, the first thing we need to do is speak the truth in a way that enables them to hear God's point of view. This will bring encouragement to them and build them up. Kingdom virtue should be reflected in our voice.

Now, I'm not talking about turning every conversation into a sermon. What I am talking about is giving people a perspective that is rooted and grounded in a God-centered point of view as opposed to a world-centered point of view. We shouldn't be agreeing with the world when the world is disagreeing with God.

Nor are we to let sympathy cancel the truth. That seems to be at an all-time high. We are being shamed into agreeing with lies. While hate speech does exist, not every disagreeing statement is hate speech. And yet because there are many people who do not like the truth, they are using shame as a way of backing people away from speaking the truth. As a kingdom disciple, you should never back away from truth, and certainly not out of a desire for acceptance. Let God be true and every man a liar (Romans 3:4).

We are to be people of the truth. You and I are to know, understand, apply, and speak God's perspective on every matter we are facing. Truth isn't something relegated to preachers. It is to flow from believer to believer and saint to saint. That's how we are to encourage each other in a day and age that applauds the destruction of Christian values at all costs.

Have you ever been to the zoo and seen a wild animal in a cage? The reason they have the wild animal behind bars is because it is dangerous. Similarly, the tongue is dangerous. That is why the tongue comes caged in what we call a mouth, behind some bars we call our teeth. Yes, the tongue can be a tool for transformation and impact, but far too often it is used as a tool to tear down. We are to speak truth, but we are to speak it with a heart of love. Truth must always be delivered with love.

One of God's greatest attributes is love. It's part of His innate being. God *is* love. Yet so many of us don't fully grasp what love means. It's a word that is often thrown around in a nonchalant way. So let me define love biblically. *Love* is "the decision to compassionately, righteously, and responsibly seek the well-being of another." It is a decision, not only a feeling. The reason I say it is a decision is because it is commanded by God. A command demands obedience. Love always starts off with a decision. It is a decision to compassionately, righteously, and responsibly do or say something for the betterment of someone else.

This means we are to speak the truth so that the person we're speaking to knows we are saying what we are saying to achieve what is best for them—because we want what will be good for them. Obviously, venting would not fall in that category. Neither would gossip, insults, or insinuations. When you and I communicate, according to God's standards on speech, we must communicate in a way that seeks to help—to make something, or someone, better. People should know how much we care for their well-being when we communicate with them.

Now, that doesn't mean we are to dumb down the truth, but neither does it mean we are to eradicate any concern. When you come across believers who you know are believing or living or saying something errant—who are sinning—they need to know the truth, yes. But they also need to know that the reason you are telling them the truth is because you care for them and are seeking to keep them from the consequences of an errant way. You are directing them toward God's perspective on the matter in a way that is seasoned with grace.

LOVE IS GREATER THAN TOLERANCE

Love does not tolerate all views. Love does not acquiesce to lies. Christians are to love all people, but we are not called to love all ideas. God draws a clear difference between the sin and the sinner. God loves the sinner. He does not love the sin. Neither does He conflate the two. For example, a loving parent does not accept the wrong behavior of their child, and yet they still love their child. And if they are a good parent, they treat their child with love even when they have to correct them. We are always to make a distinction between the action and the person.

> **Love does not tolerate all views. Love does not acquiesce to lies. Christians are to love all people, but we are not called to love all ideas.**

We are to love the immoral person. We are not to love immorality. We are to love the people of different races. We are not to love racism. We are to love the angry person. We are not to love anger. The problem today is that the world has attempted to shut down biblical influence in our culture by conflating the sinner and the sin. They are saying that to reject a sin makes you intolerant. But we are never to be intolerant toward another person made in the image of God. Yet we are also never to deny the truth out of a desire for acceptance. We are to speak the truth in love so that people know we care about their well-being.

You should never have to choose between truth and love.

If we are going to live as people with kingdom virtue, we must always speak truth with love. When we fail to do that and only speak truth, it comes across like hitting people with a hammer or beating them up. Even when it is accurate information, if it is not given in a spirit and context of love, it can feel judgmental.

On the other hand, if you try to live by offering love with no truth, all you are doing is condoning a culture that has chosen to leave out God. You are helping people to feel good about a lie. You are enabling them by making them feel good about something they should feel bad about. That is not your role as a kingdom disciple. Your role isn't to help people feel better about the lie. Your role is to help them get better as you encourage or inspire them to choose to live in truth.

Unfortunately, today we have a society that promotes believing lies in the name of love. We've got confused Christians getting into the mix as well, having a damaging effect on God's interactions with believers today—not only personally but collectively as well.

Most people do not realize this, but God will use your tongue, and how you handle the truth in love, to determine how much of Him you get to experience in this life. Matthew 12:34–37 tells us that every word we say is being recorded. We are being held accountable for every word. That's why it is so important to set a guard over your mouth and a watch over your lips, as the psalmist writes poetically in Psalm 141:3. Because when you don't and you allow your words to run wild, you are hindering your own spiritual growth, as well as the spiritual growth of others.

Rather than erect a barrier between ourselves and God, we ought to look for ways to draw closer to Him. That's how we grow. That's how we develop kingdom virtues and overcome chaos through character. First John 4 reveals to us that when we live in truth and love, speaking it with our words and intentions, God reveals more of himself to us, perfecting His love in us. He does this so that as we abide in Him more and more, we then reveal more of His love to others. It's a cycle. We read,

- ▸ "Beloved, let us love one another, for love is from God; and everyone who loves is born of God and knows God" (v. 7).
- ▸ "No one has seen God at any time; if we love one another, God abides in us, and His love is perfected in us" (v. 12).
- ▸ "By this we know that we abide in Him and He in us, because He has given us of His Spirit" (v. 13).
- ▸ "We have come to know and have believed the love which God has for us. God is love, and the one who abides in love abides in God, and God abides in him" (v. 16).

► "There is no fear in love; but perfect love casts out fear, because fear involves punishment, and the one who fears is not perfected in love" (v. 18).

► "And this commandment we have from Him, that the one who loves God should love his brother also" (v. 21).

Merging the sharing of truth with love opens the doorway to a greater experience of God in your life. And couldn't we all use more of the greatness of God in our lives? God's presence casts out fear and calms the chaos. God's presence ushers in peace, hope, and joy. God allows you and me to feel more of His love when He sees that we are willing to share His love and His truth with others.

What's more, when you and I make it our lifestyle to live with kingdom virtues on the foundation of truth merged with a spirit of love, aligning our will with God's, more of our prayers are answered. As we reflect God more in what we say and how we say it, God is more attuned to our prayers. Now, so that you don't think I'm making that up, let me show you where it says that in 1 John 3:18–22. We read,

Little children, let us not love with word or with tongue, but in deed and truth. We will know by this that we are of the truth, and will assure our heart before Him in whatever our heart condemns us; for God is greater than our heart and knows all things. Beloved, if our heart does not condemn us, we have confidence before God; and whatever we ask we receive from Him, because we keep His commandments and do the things that are pleasing in His sight.

One of the best ways to get your prayers answered is to merge truth with love. That means you cannot be a silo saint. You can't be a stay-at-home follower of Jesus Christ. And I'm not talking about just going to church or to a sanctuary either. You need to be engaged with others on a regular basis so that you first have the opportunity to speak the truth in love. When you are touching people and

87

encouraging them to build kingdom virtue in their lives, God sees that you are doing that which is "pleasing in His sight."

So many people feel free today to go on social media and correct, judge, teach, or blame people they might not even know. But truth spoken in a spirit and context of love most often happens in an environment of relationship. In order to have relationships, you need to intentionally connect with others. You have to know people well enough to know when the truth might be needed in their lives. You can't do that if you are never around anybody. The church has many purposes, and one of them is to provide for fellowship among believers.

Far too many people wound up using COVID-19 as an excuse not to attend church once the lockdown lifted. They found it far too convenient to watch a sermon on YouTube and call it a day. But church was never meant to simply be a sermon dispenser, like a Redbox where you get DVDs. Church is a place to connect with others in such a way that everyone can experience God together as we serve Him and get to know Him, and each other, better.

What's more, when you are involved in the lives of people—and you allow people to be involved in your life as well—you are given opportunities to speak the truth in love. You don't have to demand that your voice be heard. You don't have to shout—or use all caps.

God has given us a community in which we can all thrive, when we come together on the basis of two foundational virtues of truth and love. Jesus merged these two (truth and love) in a unique sermon He preached to His followers, on a mountainside by the Sea of Galilee. He spent this sermon speaking on what it means to live with kingdom values. The remainder of our time in these pages will be spent on a journey through this sermon, as we take a deeper look into how God defines kingdom values, and how we are to express them in our own lives.

PART TWO

THE COMPONENTS OF BIBLICAL CHARACTER

7

POOR IN SPIRIT

The Sermon on the Mount is the greatest sermon ever preached by the greatest preacher who ever lived. Jesus Christ proclaimed this masterpiece. We have come to know the qualities He spoke on in this sermon as the Beatitudes. But when we look more closely at His message, we can see that Jesus is solidly outlining how to live with kingdom values as His kingdom followers. Whether you want to refer to these attributes as beatitudes or as kingdom values, living according to them will reflect the King of Kings and bring Him glory and will bring us good.

We are introduced to the setting of this powerful message in the first two verses of Matthew 5, where we read, "When Jesus saw the crowds, He went up on the mountain; and after He sat down, His disciples came to Him. He opened His mouth and began to teach them, saying . . ."

Notice that there are two groups here. There are the disciples, to whom He's directly speaking. And there is the multitude who have gathered nearby to overhear His conversation with the disciples. Essentially, Jesus is speaking to both groups in His Sermon on the Mount: the masses and His followers.

It's a bit like when I prepare to preach at the church I pastor, Oak Cliff Bible Fellowship. I'll write the sermon with our congregation in mind. I use phrases and nuances that resonate with the shared history and faith of our members. I might even target certain applications based on my personal knowledge of what we, as a congregation, are going through at that time.

Once I've preached in the church to my congregation, my words go beyond that pulpit when our national ministry, the Urban Alternative, takes my Sunday sermons and airs them on radio, on television, and online. Through the Urban Alternative's distribution, what started as a localized message delivered to local church members now broadens into a global message reaching the masses.

Similarly, when Jesus spoke to His disciples on the mountain that day, He chose and shaped His message to elevate them to a higher level of kingdom discipleship. But what was relevant to them was also relevant to the people gathered nearby, and it remains relevant to anyone who has heard or will hear it throughout time—through today and beyond.

We know that Jesus was aiming for increased levels of kingdom discipleship in His hearers because the values He spoke on are bracketed by "for theirs is the kingdom of heaven" statements on both sides. We read this phrase in verse 3, the opening of His message, and again in the closing of His focus on these values in verse 10.

Jesus starts and ends His emphasis on kingdom-based values with this phrase, and it is obvious that, in His teaching on how to live as His followers, He wants to share with His disciples the concept of the kingdom. He tells them what the kingdom is, how the kingdom works, and how they can benefit from the kingdom in being blessed by it. He instructs them on the cause-and-effect nature of kingdom living. Jesus calls the positive resulting state "blessed" throughout.

In fact, in the first twelve verses of His Sermon on the Mount, Jesus uses the word *blessed* nine times. With each usage, we discover what we need to do (what kingdom values we need to live by) in order to receive kingdom blessings. These nine references to blessings cover eight specific values that God desires for us to live by. One of the values has a double blessing associated with it, but we will get to that later in the book.

The main idea, though, as we start on our journey through these kingdom values, is that living according to them brings about blessing. Jesus wants each of us to know that choosing to embrace kingdom values isn't just something you do so you can check off a list. It isn't just something you do so you can post virtue-signaling statements online. Neither is it about grinning and bearing it as you seek to live the Christian life.

Rather, Jesus pairs each of these kingdom values with a blessing that comes right back to you. Instead of living a life of chaos, you'll discover calm. Instead of wandering aimlessly in pain, you will find comfort. Instead of going through life unsatisfied, you will find what you need when you need it most. In these eight statements on kingdom values, Jesus also provides the purpose behind living them out. He gives us an incentive, reminding us that when we choose to live and be shaped according to kingdom values, we will be accessing the blessings of God's kingdom for ourselves.

The kingdom values Jesus spoke on in the Sermon on the Mount outline both the responsibility and the benefits of living in the kingdom.

LOOKING WITHIN

Throughout His sermon, Jesus addresses the major problem the people of His day faced, one that people also face today: looking at life from the outside only. The worst thing you can do is view your life from the outside, because the stuff you have, the status you have reached, the house you live in, or the car you drive does not determine your level of blessing in this life. You probably know people who have a lot of things but who are miserable on the inside.

That might even be you. But a life of kingdom living that produces kingdom blessing allows you to experience the benefits of the kingdom internally.

It'll help us as we set out to walk through these values to define the term *blessed* from a biblical standpoint. *Blessed* describes "a state of well-being where kingdom followers of Christ both enjoy and extend the goodness of God in their lives." And "state of well-being" refers to your normal way of being, not a moment of happiness here or a burst of energy or enthusiasm there. It's a way of life, not an event.

This state of well-being and divine favor and spiritual stability, also known as "joy" in Scripture, is referred to in the Bible as an inner river that keeps flowing even in times of drought. It is the work of the Holy Spirit to produce this in a believer's life. Part of our role in fostering our own growth and maturity is choosing to live by the kingdom values outlined for us in the Word of God.

> Part of our role in fostering our own growth and maturity is choosing to live by the kingdom values outlined for us in the Word of God.

A Christian who is joyless, if that is his or her normal state, is not very close with the Holy Spirit. Because when you and I abide in Christ, and thus abide in His Spirit, it is the role of the Spirit to fill us with that inner river—the water flowing over with joy.

The Greek word translated as "blessed" in the Sermon on the Mount is the word *Makarios*. This name referred to an island off the coast of Greece known at that time as the "blessed island." It was called blessed because it was self-sustained. The residents there didn't have to leave the island to get anything because the island offered everything they could ever need. The natural resources of this blessed island were so rich, fruitful, productive, and bountiful that the islanders had all they needed to enjoy their lives to the fullest.

In the biblical concept of being blessed, you will discover all you need to live a fulfilled and satisfied life—and you ought to be okay living on an island. Just being with the King surrounded by His kingdom should stir up within you an awareness of how blessed you are. But far too many believers today feel the urge to go somewhere, to buy something, or to change homes, jobs, mates, cars, or churches in a constant search for something external to satisfy them, rather than remaining content on the island of God's kingdom blessings.

One of the ways you know that you are not blessed in the biblical sense is that you have to keep leaving the island to have any amount of satisfaction. You have to leave the island to find peace or happiness or to feel significant. Anyone who does not recognize what they have with Christ and His kingdom blessings will have to leave the island in a constant search for more.

If you find yourself running all around town trying to find your blessing or experience your blessing, you are looking in the wrong location. As a kingdom follower of Jesus Christ, you already have access to your blessing within. You are already on the island called "blessed." You just need to open your spiritual eyes and discover what God has for you. You need to comprehend that there is a cause-and-effect aspect to kingdom blessings.

Living according to kingdom values leads to a life filled with kingdom blessings. It's as simple, and as difficult, as that. I say that it is simple because it is pretty straightforward. There aren't any hoops to jump through. But it is also difficult because we make it so through our rebellion, stubbornness, and desire to find our own way.

Friend, Jesus is *the* way. He knows the way we should go in order to experience the blessings of His kingdom. Just as He spoke to His disciples on the mountainside overlooking the expansive Sea of Galilee, He speaks to us today through His message.

Not too long ago I was able to visit Israel with my family and ministry partners of the Urban Alternative. One of the highlights of the trip was going up on the mountain where Jesus sat down to teach His disciples and the mass of people gathered to hear. As I stood on the mountainside along with the film crew and my family, I took a moment to look out over the terrain and imagine what it might have looked like with everyone gathered together. I could picture Jesus sitting down on a large stone to teach and the crowd growing quiet. In case you missed it earlier, Jesus did sit down. We read that in the passage that opened this chapter. Jesus sat down when He taught on the hillside.

It could have been that Jesus sat down because He was tired. Or it might have been because He knew He was about to speak for a relatively long time. Or it could have also been symbolic. In those days, as it is in our day to a large extent, to sit and teach was to do so from a seat of authority. Like a king sitting on his throne to rule over his kingdom, or the pope speaking ex cathedra—meaning "from the chair"—or a judge presiding over a case on the bench, it means to speak from authority.

So when Jesus spoke of the kingdom values we are about to explore together through these pages, know that He did so from a position of authority. No one has more authority than He to deliver the kingdom principles by which we are to live. He is the King of Kings. He owns and rules the world we call our home. And since He does, He knows how we are to live as kingdom disciples in it.

FIRST THINGS FIRST

The first kingdom value Jesus chose to focus on shows up in verse 3. We read, "Blessed are the poor in spirit, for theirs is the kingdom of heaven." It's a short statement, but it contains a world of truth. Jesus begins by telling us we are blessed when we are poor. Now, I know that nobody in their right mind likes being poor. If you are a person who loves being poor, you've probably got a problem.

Sure, some people can't help that they are poor, but it's usually not because they want to be.

Many of us grew up poor. I did. I'm sure many of you reading this book did as well. We grew up without much at all. Some of us grew up eating mayonnaise sandwiches. A mayonnaise sandwich is just that—some bread with some mayo on it. That's all. And if your mom was finally able to get some meat to go on the sandwich, it was the bologna that would bubble up in the middle. Some of us also grew up with government-issued cheese or beans or powdered milk.

I'm sure there are those of you reading this book who know exactly what I'm talking about. And I am sure you didn't exactly want to be in the condition you were in at that time. You wanted something better, more freedom and the means to progress in life. You wanted something more comfortable than being enmeshed in poverty. And no one would blame you for that.

But that's not the poverty Jesus spoke about. Jesus spoke on a spiritual poverty. What's more, He spoke of it in a way that declared this spiritual poverty to be absolutely essential. He started His revolutionary sermon by saying something revolutionary to everyone listening at that time, and still today: "Blessed are the poor in spirit." That last part of the phrase is key. Jesus was pronouncing a blessing on spiritual poverty. He wasn't condemning money. He wasn't condemning the acquisition of land, animals, or even stuff for a home.

In fact, many of God's choicest servants in Scripture were wealthy by today's standards. Many would be considered multimillionaires today. Abraham would have fit into that category, as would David, and Job. There was even at least one billionaire in there too, Solomon. God had no problem with giving His people financial prosperity in the Bible.

But what He did and does have a problem with, as indicated by Jesus' opening statement, is when people use their stuff—their wealth—to measure their spiritual status. For someone to think that because they have a nice car God must be close to them or must love them more than the next person is to be deceived and void of the true values of the kingdom. To assume, just because someone has a better job than the average Joe, that God favors them more than others or that God is on their side, is to have missed the meaning of life itself. A person can be very successful in the physical realm and yet be one of God's worst enemies. Material success does not equate to spiritual success. Sometimes the two coincide, but that is not always the case and should never be assumed.

Jesus reminded His disciples and the others listening that to be blessed in God's kingdom means to intentionally embrace a life that is poor in spirit. The Greek word translated as "poor" in this passage referred to a beggar in New Testament times. It referred to someone who would ask for the crumbs from a rich man's table because they were so destitute (see Luke 16:19–31). Someone who was poor couldn't take care of their own basic needs. They did not possess the physical resources to feed, clothe, or house themselves, so they literally depended on charity to get by. They were beggars.

> **A person who is poor in spirit understands that if God doesn't act out of charity and give them what they need to live life as it is meant to be lived, they are going to starve to death spiritually.**

If someone didn't extend help to a beggar, especially in the days in which Jesus taught, they simply wouldn't make it. Jesus didn't use a moderate term for *poor*. He used the most extreme term possible in order to make His point.

His point was that to be "poor in spirit" means that a person recognizes they do not possess in their own human capacity the ability to live life as the Creator meant it to be lived. A person who is poor in spirit understands that if God doesn't act out of charity and give them what they need to live life as it is meant to be lived, they are going to starve to death spiritually. They are going to wither and waste away spiritually.

This person knows that the "nothing" written in John 15:5, "apart from Me you can do nothing," truly means *nothing*.

Jesus wasn't whistling Dixie that day when He led off with a blessing on spiritual poverty. He wasn't just throwing down a sermonette to get people to clap. He was making it crystal clear that when it comes to living life as life was meant to be lived, a person must be poor in spirit.

As people, we do not possess the spiritual capacity to address our own spiritual needs. The problem is that we often forget or ignore that. We flip it and say, "Blessed are the rich in spirit" or the "strong of heart." We applaud independence, self-confidence, and oftentimes even pride. But Jesus says if that is how you choose to live, you can flip the consequences too. Instead of being blessed, you will be living in the realm of darkness. By placing yourself in the authoritative position of Christ and His rule in your life, you are choosing to let go of your blessing.

Paul summarized this kingdom value of being poor in spirit when he wrote,

> If anyone else has a mind to put confidence in the flesh, I far more.
> . . . But whatever things were gain to me, those things I have counted
> as loss for the sake of Christ. More than that, I count all things to
> be loss in view of the surpassing value of knowing Christ Jesus my
> Lord, for whom I have suffered the loss of all things, and count
> them but rubbish so that I may gain Christ, and may be found in
> Him, not having a righteousness of my own derived from the Law,
> but that which is through faith in Christ, the righteousness which
> comes from God on the basis of faith.
>
> Philippians 3:4, 7–9

Paul's material and personal success were nothing more than rubbish to him when placed against the backdrop of knowing Jesus Christ as Lord. That's a true reflection of a kingdom disciple who is poor in spirit. Paul recognized that he had no resources of his own when it came to living the successful spiritual life. If he was going to enjoy spiritual success at all, it would have to come through his relationship with Jesus Christ and the righteousness that would flow to him on the basis of faith.

To be poor in spirit is to declare spiritual bankruptcy. Oftentimes, when a person is unable to pay for what they have, they file bankruptcy. Similarly, to live according to the kingdom value of being poor in spirit comes through recognizing our insufficiency to satisfy what is needed for us to prosper spiritually.

Now, it's not hard to recognize if you can't pay your bills. But most of us have a hard time realizing we don't have what it takes to make ends meet spiritually. We can't provide what is needed for us to mature spiritually, be impactful, access blessings, and prosper in our souls. Unfortunately, most of us believe we are far more capable than we actually are. This keeps us on the hamster wheel, spinning in cycles of reading our Bible, attending church, or crossing off our prayer lists—only to discover we aren't making any progress.

But Jesus didn't start out His sermon by saying, "Blessed are those who cross off their spiritual lists." No, He began with "Blessed are the poor in spirit, for theirs is the kingdom of heaven."

YOU GET THE KINGDOM

In the Greek text, the word translated "theirs" is in the emphatic position. That means *theirs* refers to those who are poor in spirit and nobody else. Only the poor in spirit get to experience the kingdom of heaven. If you are not poor in spirit because you are rich in self-confidence, then you don't get the kingdom of heaven. If you are not poor in spirit because you rely too heavily on your position, power, or prosperity on earth, you don't get the kingdom. Only those who are poor in spirit get the kingdom—its benefits, blessings, and experiences on earth.

If you've listened to me at all, or if you've read any of my books, you'll know that I am highly focused on the kingdom in my studies and teachings. I believe that the main thread stretching throughout Scripture is God's kingdom and our relationship to it. The Greek word translated "kingdom" is *basileia*. It refers to rule or authority. In any kingdom, you only have one ultimate ruler. If there are two who believe they are the ultimate ruler, you will have a civil war because a kingdom can only be ruled by one king.

In the kingdom of heaven, God is the king, which makes Him the ruler. It is our role to align our lives under His overarching rule. What Jesus is emphasizing in this opening kingdom value is that when we do that, we tap into the authority and power of the kingdom. We get to access kingdom rule on earth. And because God created the earth, His rule overrules any others attempting to be in charge here.

Jesus summarized it like this: "These things I have spoken to you, so that in Me you may have peace. In the world you have tribulation, but take courage; I have overcome the world" (John 16:33). How did Jesus overcome the world? By operating from a different kingdom. And when you and I are poor in spirit, we can overcome this world, and the troubles of this world, because the overruling power of the kingdom of heaven will be made accessible to us.

More and more these days, it seems like this world is seeking to overrule our personal decisions. We can sense the stranglehold of humanity's rule creeping in. But Jesus says that if we will recognize that our spiritual strength and abilities are rooted and grounded in Him—because we are poor in spirit—then we will be able to overcome the myriad of things that seem to be coming at us.

Whether it is depression, feelings of defeat, isolation, grief, or even just a sense of aimlessness—whatever it is can be overcome. It is overcome by Christ in you when you recognize His complete sufficiency as King and Lord of all. Earth, this realm, may tell you there's no hope. Earth may tell you that you will be depressed or a failure for the rest of your life. Earth may tell you there is no future for you. But what you must remember, if you are poor in spirit, is that earth doesn't have the last word. God does. And whatever Satan is using to seek to overcome you, God can overcome it when you look to Him to do it.

In most athletic competitions, the highest score wins—whether it's football, baseball, basketball, or tennis. But that is not the case in golf. In golf, the low score wins. You can't finish up a game of golf and get excited because you have the most points. It's the low score that rules on the golf greens.

Now, in our world's value systems, it's the person with the highest accolades who seems to win. People with the highest status, the highest income, or the highest notoriety seem to win.

But Jesus says in this sermon that as long as you think you are the high man on this field called earth, you are not going to be the true winner. Because in the kingdom of heaven, the low score wins. Humility wins. Gentleness wins. The merciful person wins. The poor in spirit wins. The person who understands and recognizes that Jesus Christ is the source and sustainer of all things wins. They win by accessing the authority of the kingdom of heaven in the muck and mess of this world.

First Peter 5:6 says, "Therefore humble yourselves under the mighty hand of God, that He may exalt you at the proper time." When you and I choose to bow low before God, it is He who then lifts us up when the time comes to do so. Now, either you can bow low yourself, or God can help you. God doesn't mind helping a brother or a sister out when it comes to bowing low before Him. He can create or allow situations that you cannot fix in your humanity no matter how much money or power you have, or how many people you know. You won't be able to run from the situation. And even when you think you have fixed it, it will probably break down again.

Scripture sometimes refers to this as "brokenness." Brokenness, also known as the wilderness, is those seasons or situations that God uses in a believer's life to remind him or her of who God is, and who isn't God.

Oftentimes, when God puts you in a situation like this to teach you humility and dependence upon Him, it is like quicksand—the harder you try to fix it yourself, the deeper you will sink. It is in times like these when many people start to question God. They start to wonder if God hates them, or if He is against them. But when God puts us in a situation we cannot fix, He is doing us a favor. He is showing us our insufficiency so that we can see the kingdom of heaven at work on our behalf.

I know it may be a painful sort of favor. It can also be an inconvenient one. But when God is trying to get you and me to live with the kingdom value of being poor in spirit, it is a divine favor. Because once we know enough to declare spiritual bankruptcy, He opens His storehouses of provision to meet us where we need Him most.

There is one clear way to tell the difference between those who are living in a spiritually self-sufficient manner and those who have adopted and applied the kingdom value of being poor in spirit. Those who are poor in spirit give thanks rather than complain. When a person's gratitude is more frequent than their grumbling, it signifies that they understand the kingdom value of being poor in spirit.

After the exodus, the children of Israel experienced God's parting of the Red Sea for them to cross on dry ground, but a short time later they began to complain of a lack of water in the wilderness. They had forgotten that the same God who can part the water can provide the water. Instead of remaining in a spirit of thanks, they quickly devolved into a spirit of complaints. When complaining marks a person, he or she is not poor in spirit. That person is not entirely dependent upon God and trusting God to meet his or her needs.

Have you ever gotten on a scale, but you couldn't handle the truth of the number staring back at you? So you set about to fix it. You shifted a little to the right or leaned on the wall just a bit, to shave off a pound or two. We lean because we don't want the scale to reflect the truth of our weight.

A lot of believers today don't want to see the truth of their spiritual poverty, so they camouflage it with a façade of stuff, perhaps a façade of religious activity, friends, or even family—never getting around to what God really wants them to see: the truth of their own insufficiency. It is only in recognizing this truth and applying it to your life that you will be on your way to living in the blessings of the kingdom of heaven.

8

MOURNING

I've had my fair share of mourning and grief. In a two-year span, I lost seven family members to various forms of disease and illness. I have become all too familiar with what mourning feels like and what it can produce in the state of our emotions, thoughts, and even focus. When someone mourns, they do not do so for a moment. Mourning encompasses the entirety of that time or season. It might not be evident in every action, but it hovers as a cloud or takes up residence as a fog, affecting the movements of life.

As pastor of a large congregation, I also regularly walk with people through what seems to be more than their fair share. Grief has become a part of life for many of us. Especially with the onset of the global pandemic, it has become increasingly difficult not to come across someone you know who is either fighting a serious illness or mourning the loss of someone they love. More and more people have discovered in this season of sorrow that we are totally dependent on God to satisfy the needs of our souls. We become blessed when we recognize our spiritual inadequacy, particularly as it relates to this area of mourning, sorrow, and loss.

Jesus addressed the topic of mourning in His Sermon on the Mount, but what He said might surprise you. Anyone who has grieved knows the toll it can take on your ability to think clearly, to function fully, and even to get through some days. I'm fairly certain no one considers mourning a positive thing. Most of us live with the hope that we can somehow avoid it. But Jesus spoke of this process in a whole new way, connecting it to something different than we might expect when we hear the term. As we study His kingdom perspective, it will enable each of us to alter our own perspective of what it means to mourn in a way that brings God glory and us good.

We read of His next kingdom value that "Blessed are those who mourn, for they shall be comforted" (Matthew 5:4). If we were to change this statement into terms we often use today, it might say, "Blessed are those who are sad, or those who are despondent, for they will be comforted." In whatever ways we change the terms, though, most people hearing this would still be confused by how the words *blessed* and *mourning*, *sad*, or even *despondent* can show up together in the same sentence.

After all, we live in a fun, entertainment-based culture. Most of us want to plow right through any grief or sadness we experience. We prefer to get through it quickly so that we don't have to endure it for any length of time. This is because in our society, laughter is what is loved. Excitement is what is emphasized. And it is often encouraged that any form of sorrow be medicated right away. Enjoyment has become one of our premiere idols.

And yet Jesus says we are blessed if we cry. We are comforted when we grieve. We gain spiritually when we mourn.

But how can that be? If we read His statement without further study, it could leave us confused because it is so completely opposite of what our culture pushes and seeks. Because of that, many of us simply skip over this portion of His sermon on kingdom values, similar to how we seek to skip past any process of grief or mourning. But what I want to encourage us to do is to look at it more closely. Because when we look at the contextual environment of the culture in which Jesus spoke, we find a lot more to this verse than meets the eye.

Second Corinthians 7:8–10 gives greater insight into the full meaning of mourning during the days Jesus walked on earth. To mourn doesn't only refer to grieving the loss of a loved one, as we often associate it today. Neither does it only refer to grieving the loss of something, such as a dream, a relationship, or a way of life. To mourn something involves feeling sorrow over it.

It could be compared to what many people went through, and many are still going through, when the pandemic hit. Many of us grieved the loss of what we once depended on as normalcy and even predictability. We probably wouldn't call it mourning, but those are the feelings many experienced at the sudden changes. Weddings were postponed, vacations canceled, family birthday parties prevented from taking place as they used to. Each of these losses, stacked up on each other, created a grief we felt inside.

These feelings were sometimes referred to as "social isolation depression," but essentially, we mourned. We grieved the loss of routine. Mourning and grief can surround many things in our lives, not just the death of a loved one. And once we expand our thoughts on what mourning means, as well as what it can produce in us when we cooperate with the process spiritually, we can begin to look at other passages in Scripture that speak to sorrow. We can discover in more detail what Jesus referred to when He urged us all to live with the kingdom value known as mourning.

SORROW THAT PRODUCES SOMETHING

In biblical times, mourning frequently referred to a person's grief over their own personal sin, or the corporate sin of a body of individuals. Paul echoes this connection of mourning to sin when he writes in 2 Corinthians 7:8–10,

> For though I caused you sorrow by my letter, I do not regret it; though I did regret it—for I see that that letter caused you sorrow, though only for a while—I now rejoice, not that you were made

sorrowful, but that you were made sorrowful to the point of repentance; for you were made sorrowful according to the will of God, so that you might not suffer loss in anything through us. For the sorrow that is according to the will of God produces a repentance without regret, leading to salvation, but the sorrow of the world produces death.

In this passage, Paul refers to a sorrow tied to the will of God, not a sorrow tied to the world or circumstances. It is a sorrow that leads to repentance. That right there begins to clarify for us what Jesus was speaking about.

In the Bible, there is only one thing a person repents from, and that is sin. Thus, Paul speaks of a sorrow related to the presence of sin in the life of a believer. Essentially, Jesus states that those who are sad over the presence of sin operating in their lives will be blessed. Or another way of stating it might be "Blessed are those who are sad to the point of going to God and repenting because of the presence and impact of sin in their lives."

> **Essentially, Jesus states that those who are sad over the presence of sin operating in their lives will be blessed.**

Worldly sorrow comes tied to the consequences of sin in a person's life. This occurs whether a person is a Christian or not. Nobody wants the negative repercussions that come from bad decisions. That's a natural sorrow felt by anyone who has to pay the piper for the wrong choices they've made. But that's not the kind of sorrow Paul writes about.

Paul refers to a sorrow not created by consequences. Rather, he writes of a sorrow created by the cause itself. In other words, the sorrow is over the sin that caused the consequences and simultaneously saddened the heart of God. This is the sorrow that can bring about blessing in a person's life.

An important thing we need to understand about God is that one of His chief attributes and characteristics is holiness. He is distinctly holy. Holiness means to be set apart. God exists separate from sin. To God, sin is similar to what rotten garbage is to us. No one would want to live in an environment of rotten, smelly garbage or seek to stay there. It wouldn't be pleasant because it has a stench to it. If it were piled up in every room in your home, you would either get rid of it or look for another place to live, because living with the stench of garbage, as well as what rotten garbage attracts—rats, ants, flies, and more—would prove to be unsanitary and a health hazard. Unacceptable.

That's why we take our garbage out so it can get picked up and delivered to a garbage collection location. Or if you live in an area without garbage pickup, you probably have a pit where you burn it and bury it over time. If you are a parent, you have probably urged your kids to clean their room because you don't want them living with mess or garbage. None of us takes any delight in hanging out with garbage, whether it is our own or someone else's.

But when sin is operating in the life of a believer, he or she is asking a holy God to hang out with garbage. They are saying that even though they know that Christ lives in them in the presence of the Holy Spirit, they aren't going to address or remove the filth of sin in their lives. Basically, they are telling God to get used to the smell.

When Jesus gave us the kingdom value of mourning, He was telling us that we are blessed when we have inner anguish over the garbage we've allowed in our lives. We are blessed when we mourn the garbage allowed in the world. We are blessed when we experience sadness for the sinful garbage present in the lives of those we love and fellow believers in Christ. Blessed is the one who is not comfortable with their own or this world's contaminated garbage.

We have a tragedy today in our culture, and that is found in more and more people mourning less and less, if at all, over sin. They are excusing sin. They are procrastinating about dealing with sin. They are calling sinful thoughts and behaviors anything but sin. What's worse, they are applauding the ringleaders and promoters of sinful ideologies, sinful actions, and sinful values. You know that people hate sin less today than ever, or in my lifetime at least, because they ignore it more. Behavior that shouldn't be funny is laughed at now. Stuff that would make God blush is considered cute now.

Yet despite our collective change in how we view sin as a Christian culture, God has not changed. Sin still offends Him. Sin still saddens Him. Sin still carries a stench to Him. So while we may be laughing or sweeping sin under the rug, God is crying over it. And if God is crying, yet we're not feeling it, that means we have drifted so far from God that we no longer hurt as He hurts, or sense what He sees. Rather, we have become accustomed to this world of darkness rather than the kingdom of light.

Our distance from God doesn't come without consequences. A loss of fellowship with God results in a loss of blessing from God. In God, there exists no darkness at all. So if you are content to remain in darkness rather than be purified through repentance and the turning away from sin in your life, you are choosing to forfeit the many spiritual blessings God has for you.

Now, I'm not suggesting that a person does not sin if he or she is a Christian. We all sin and fall short of the glory of God (Romans 3:23). But if you are walking in fellowship with God, you will feel sorrow for your sin. The sin will cause you anguish and pain, for a number of reasons. But a primary reason is because it has broken your intimate fellowship with God.

When Jesus tells us that we are blessed when we live by the kingdom value of mourning, we are to understand that we are blessed when we recognize that our sin, or the sin in this world even, has hurt the heart of God. When Jesus looked out over Jerusalem and wept (Luke 19:41), he mourned the people's sin of rejecting Him and rejecting God, the Father who sent Him; He was mourning the sinful state of an entire group of people. From Luke 13:34 we get insight:

O Jerusalem, Jerusalem, the city that kills the prophets and stones those sent to her! How often I wanted to gather your children together, just as a hen gathers her brood under her wings, and you would not have it!

Other instances recorded in Scripture clearly demonstrate the relationship between mourning and sin. Here are a few of them:

- "The LORD said to him, 'Go through the midst of the city, even through the midst of Jerusalem, and put a mark on the foreheads of the men who sigh and groan over all the abominations which are being committed in its midst'" (Ezekiel 9:4).
- "Righteousness belongs to You, O Lord, but to us open shame, as it is this day—to the men of Judah, the inhabitants of Jerusalem and all Israel, those who are nearby and those who are far away in all the countries to which You have driven them, because of their unfaithful deeds which they have committed against You. Open shame belongs to us, O Lord, to our kings, our princes and our fathers, because we have sinned against You" (Daniel 9:7–8)
- "Then I said, 'Woe is me, for I am ruined! Because I am a man of unclean lips, and I live among a people of unclean lips; for my eyes have seen the King, the LORD of hosts'" (Isaiah 6:5).
- "My eyes shed streams of water, because they do not keep Your law" (Psalm 119:136).
- "'Yet even now,' declares the LORD, 'Return to Me with all your heart, and with fasting, weeping and mourning; and rend your heart and not your garments.' Now return to the LORD your God, for He is gracious and compassionate, slow to anger, abounding in lovingkindness and relenting of evil" (Joel 2:12–13).

▸ "I am afraid that when I come again my God may humiliate me before you, and I may mourn over many of those who have sinned in the past and not repented of the impurity, immorality and sensuality which they have practiced" (2 Corinthians 12:21).

▸ "Wretched man that I am! Who will set me free from the body of this death?" (Romans 7:24).

People who are close to God mourn over their sin. So if your sins—or the sins of this world—are just a blip on your radar and are not causing you to feel pain, I can assure you that you are not close to God. God mourns over the sins of His children. It's a very cold person who sees somebody they love crying and just says, "That's tough." To know the anguish our sin causes God, and the extent He went to in order to cover our sin so we can be made right with Him through the blood of Jesus Christ, and then to just shrug it off is not the mark of an authentic kingdom disciple. It shows that a person is lacking in kingdom virtue.

Sin doesn't mess with just your life, either. Sin messes with other people's lives too. Your sin carries consequences. The sins that are often applauded in our culture carry consequences as well. To ignore this reality is to ignore God and the truth of His Word. Yet we live in a day when people don't want to hear that truth. They just want to hear how much God loves them and how He is going to bless them by giving them a new car or a new house or a new job. But what many have forgotten is that the blessings are tied to intimacy. And the intimacy is tied to the condition of our heart. Mourning sin in your life, or the collective sin at large in a culture or the body of Christ, enables you to draw closer to God.

I understand this isn't a popular message. People want to hear about happy things. As a result, we tend to laugh at sin, or ignore it—or even justify it. But it is our refusal to repent from sin that hurts the heart of God. And over time, our actions that hurt God's heart also harden our own heart.

Have you ever noticed that when you sin in an area the first time, you feel it a lot more intensely than you do after you have done it many times? Your view changes as your heart hardens to the reality of the sin you are participating in. Jesus wants to remind us in emphasizing this kingdom value right at the start of His sermon that the way for you and me to be blessed by God is to live with a heart that is soft enough and sensitive enough to hurt over sin. He wants us to understand what sin does to God and what it does to prevent our relating with God in an intimate way. Another way to describe this kingdom value of mourning is *godly sorrow*. It is sorrow we feel because we know we are causing God to sorrow as well.

THE UPSIDE OF FEELING DOWN

Don't get me wrong, I'm not saying that laughter isn't called for in this life. The Bible says that a merry heart is like medicine to the soul (see Proverbs 17:22). It's just that you need to keep it in perspective. You don't want to overdose on joy. That's why the Bible says in Ecclesiastes 7:2 that a funeral is better than a party, because at a funeral you will be guided to think about what really matters and about making wiser choices in the life you still have on earth. A party merely camouflages what truly matters. But a funeral forces you to think about, evaluate, and consider how you are choosing to spend your time.

Similarly, Jesus says we need to think about, evaluate, and consider how we choose to spend our time when it comes to sin. Do we dismiss it? Do we hide it? Do we continue in it? Or do we recognize the damage it creates and acknowledge it so that we will turn from it? The psalmist David wrote about sin's lasting impact on a soul in Psalm 32:3–5, which reads,

> When I kept silent about my sin, my body wasted away
> Through my groaning all day long.
> For day and night Your hand was heavy upon me;

> My vitality was drained away as with the fever heat of
>   summer. *Selah.*
> I acknowledged my sin to You,
> And my iniquity I did not hide;
> I said, "I will confess my transgressions to the LORD";
> And You forgave the guilt of my sin. *Selah.*

David told us that as long as he didn't deal with his sin, he lived in a restless state. Yet when he dealt with it biblically—when he repented (confessed and turned away)—all of the pain and anguish he was experiencing due to it went away. You and I are blessed when we recognize our sin and what it does to the heart of God. We are blessed when we respond by confessing and repenting of our sin so that we can have restored fellowship with God.

I know that it hurts to mourn. Trust me, I know. But what Jesus assures us is that if we choose to mourn and grieve over our sin and its impact on our relationship with God, we will be comforted. We will be forgiven. We will be blessed. On the other hand, refusal to address our sin blocks our prayers from being heard and answered (see Psalm 66:18).

You and I are blessed when we recognize our sin and what it does to the heart of God. We are blessed when we respond by confessing and repenting of our sin so that we can have restored fellowship with God.

When you are in pain, you go to a doctor and tell him or her what's wrong in the hope that he or she will know what to do to bring you comfort and restored well-being. You want the doctor to turn things around. Choosing to live according to this kingdom value of mourning is no different. Blessed are those who realize they are in spiritual pain because of sin and so they go to God to restore their well-being.

The Prodigal Son received comfort from the father when he came home. He received forgiveness. One of the reasons is because he returned to his father repentant for what he had done wrong. He didn't return bragging about his disobedience and hardened by it. He returned in a state of humility and was blessed by his father as a result.

Jesus says that you also will be blessed with the comfort and love of God when you return to Him in a state of humility and mourning over your sin. You will find the comfort you need to navigate the chaos around you when you choose to call sin what it is—sin. You will find comfort when you respond to it with the anguish of a heart that seeks to honor God in all you do.

When a parent changes the dirty diaper of an infant who is crying because of the discomfort they feel due to the mess that they have made, the baby's tears turn to smiles as the loving parent cleans them, soothes them, carries them, and hugs them tight. Even so, our loving heavenly Father who is the God of all comfort releases the Holy Spirit to turn our midnight into gladness when we allow Him to clean up our mess of sin.

Humility, or being poor in spirit, lays the foundation for you to then add the kingdom value of mourning over sin in your life. These two, when paired together, open the doorway to greater blessing, peace, and well-being. They get you started on your way to fulfilling your personal spiritual purpose.

9

GENTLENESS

I enjoy the NFL commercials that show players blocking tackles or knocking people off the practice equipment because they hit it so hard, only to be followed up by a scene where they are eating soup given to them by their mother. These big, strapping guys who won't take any mess on the field become gentle as lambs when Mama shows up. The player hasn't lost any of his strength, power, or speed. He has not gotten rid of his motivation or willpower. None of that has changed. But now he has bridled it all in submission to a higher authority.

When most people hear the next kingdom virtue we are going to unpack in these pages, that of being gentle, they don't like it. Especially men. This is because to many people gentleness means weakness. It means being indecisive and wishy-washy. People often view the call to live a gentle life as a call to monkhood or something similar. They think gentleness means that you can't voice, or even have, an opinion—that you can't speak from your heart or stand up for what you believe in. Basically, being gentle, for many people, means living like a doormat.

But that definition of the word *gentle* would be an insult to Jesus, who is called gentle in Scripture. Being gentle does not mean a person lives a soft life, able to be run over by anyone and anything. Nothing could be further from the truth. What living out the kingdom virtue of gentleness means is that a person has learned to live with their power under control.

Gentleness is simply controlled strength.

Keep in mind, when Jesus urged His followers to live a meek and gentle life, saying that doing so would bring about blessings (Matthew 5:5), He did so at a time when the Jews were under Roman domination. The Jews were being oppressed and wanted nothing more than to get the Romans off their backs. They wanted freedom from the stranglehold of Roman rule, and they were looking for a leader who would achieve that.

What many people don't understand when they read the Bible's account of Jesus' trial before Pilate that set the stage for our first chapter is that Pilate had offered to release to the Jews either Jesus or Barabbas. The people probably chose Barabbas because he was a zealot. He was part of a group of insurgents who were trying to militarily overthrow Roman rule.

When the people called for Barabbas's release, they weren't necessarily hating on Jesus. They were demonstrating that they did not like His method of getting them free. They wanted someone who would use human power to defeat the Romans. That is why they chose Barabbas over Jesus. Jesus was just a little bit too gentle, or too meek. They wanted power unleashed, not power under control.

They didn't realize that for power to be effective, it has to be under control. You wouldn't want a doctor who was performing laser radiation surgery to remove a tumor to aim the radiation just anywhere on your body. Or even to move it around. Unleashing power without the wisdom and constraints to use it best rarely accomplishes the desired outcome. True liberation takes place when people exercise power under control in a strategic way. But the Jews didn't understand that when they openly called for Jesus' death. They looked down upon His gentleness as if it were a hindrance, not a help.

The Greek word translated as "meek" or "gentle" is *praos*. It describes the necessary balance between using power and avoiding harshness. It was a term typically used in regard to domesticated animals. If you've been to a circus, you know what this looks like with some of the strongest animals around, such as tigers, bears, or even elephants. When a professional trains these animals, they do not strip the animals of their power. Rather, they train the animals to contain their power in certain circumstances.

The concept of gentleness never refers to the loss of strength (as Superman suffers in the presence of kryptonite). Gentleness refers to taming power so that it can be surrendered to the overall goals at hand. If you have ever seen a wild stallion that has been broken, you have witnessed meekness. The broken horse has not lost its power. Rather, the horse's power is now harnessed under the control and guidance of the rider who directs it where it needs to go.

True greatness requires gentleness, strength under control, because if you cannot bring your own thoughts, words, and actions into alignment with overarching goals, then you will not be able to live up to your fullest potential. You can identify someone who lacks basic character qualities, especially meekness, because they lose control often. They become angry quickly. They mouth-off easily. They get irritated at other drivers or at people posting on social media; sometimes they even throw things at the TV. The chaos around them simply reflects the chaos within.

Gentleness, also known as humility, is such an important value to live by that Proverbs 25:28 compares the lack of it to a city about to be overrun by its enemy: "Like a city that is broken into and without walls is a man who has no control over his spirit."

Zephaniah 2:3 tells us that we are to pursue more of it: "Seek the Lord, all you humble of the earth who have carried out His ordinances; seek righteousness, seek humility. Perhaps you will be hidden in the day of the Lord's anger."

Zephaniah is writing to those who are already known as "humble of the earth." Yet he tells them to seek more humility, advising them that it will be a shield of protection for them. Regardless of strength, skill, power, education, wealth, or anything else, it is humility that identifies a person as great in God's eyes.

SUBMISSION TO GOD

The kingdom value of gentleness has nothing to do with submitting to anyone and everyone around you. It has to do with yielding to the legitimate authority over you, which is God, and seeking to align all you think, do, and say under the overarching rule of God in every area of your life.

One of the greatest challenges I have when it comes to counseling as a pastor is the overwhelming number of people who seem unwilling to submit to God's spiritual authority. I can explain the biblical principles relevant to whatever they are facing, but if they are not willing to apply those spiritual principles, it will have no impact. Once a person chooses to live with a rebellious spirit, that person has also chosen to cancel the work of God in their lives. The absence of humility and surrender brings chaos. The presence of humility and surrender to God brings calm. In fact, it can bring calm to such a degree that it is able to "save" or sanctify individuals in the midst of personal life struggles (see James 1:21).

A gentle person bows low before God so that he or she can stand tall among people. It is in an individual's willingness to bow before God where the greatest power can be found. The largest players on any football team are the offensive linemen. They are the biggest, strongest, and fiercest. But if you'll notice, they are also the ones who have to go to the lowest stance when it's time to run a play. The reason why they go so low and dig their knuckles into the ground is for leverage. In doing so, they access greater power.

Our culture has misunderstood gentleness to mean something it does not. It is a strategic decision and way of operating that actually gives you your greatest advantage in life. The bigger you are by this world's standards, the more meek you should be. The larger your bank account, the more gentle you should be. The broader your influence and reach, the more humble you should be. Unfortunately, it seems that the opposite occurs. With greater notoriety often comes a greater loss of personal control.

The Hoover Dam produces energy for California, Nevada, and Arizona. It is concentrated power under control. Because of this, it can produce energy for all three states. But if you ever loosed that water, it would bring disaster to the very areas it was designed to help. When power is unleashed without control, it's a tsunami. It's a torrent of chaos sweeping over and through the land, destroying everything in its way.

We've all seen people on the news or elsewhere who seem to have lost all control. It's enough to make you think they went crazy. They are doing things that are unconscionable. This is because they have lost the ability to control—or have chosen not to control—their own life force, the power they have within them.

Living with the value of gentleness translates into living with the value of self-control. You cannot have one without the other. When you and I surrender our lives to Jesus Christ, we are to surrender our gifts, skills, talents, and personal strength under the authority of God. Most of the chaos we are facing today in homes, communities, churches, and the culture is simply due to a lack of self-control and personal surrender to the legitimate authority of God's rule.

> Meekness is not weakness. Uncontrolled passions, desires, and sin are weakness. It is meekness, or gentleness, that God blesses.

Meekness is not weakness. Uncontrolled passions, desires, and sin are weakness. It is meekness, or gentleness, that God blesses. Matthew 5:5 puts it like this: "Blessed are the gentle, for they shall inherit the earth." We discover more about what it means to inherit the earth when we look at another passage found in Psalm 37. Sprinkled throughout this psalm are references to inheriting the earth or receiving the blessing of God's provision.

The psalmist begins by warning us not to become frustrated or upset when we see evil people flourish. He writes, "Do not fret because of evildoers, be not envious toward wrongdoers. For they will wither quickly like the grass and fade like the green herb" (vv. 1–2). In the beginning of this passage, we are reminded that what we see physically taking place isn't always God's endgame. It's a step in the process of God ultimately defeating evil. Those who learn how to remain self-controlled and live according to His kingdom values will experience a greater provision of His intended blessings in our lives as He carries out His will on earth.

- ▶ "Yet a little while and the wicked man will be no more; and you will look carefully for his place and he will not be there. But the humble will inherit the land and will delight themselves in abundant prosperity" (vv. 10–11).
- ▶ "For those blessed by Him will inherit the land, but those cursed by Him will be cut off" (v. 22).
- ▶ "Wait for the LORD and keep His way, and He will exalt you to inherit the land; when the wicked are cut off, you will see it" (v. 34).
- ▶ "Mark the blameless man and behold the upright; for the man of peace will have a posterity. But transgressors will be altogether destroyed; the posterity of the wicked will be cut off. But the salvation of the righteous is from the LORD; He is their strength in time of trouble. The LORD helps them and delivers them; He delivers them from the wicked and saves them, because they take refuge in Him" (vv. 37–40).

OUR INHERITANCE IN CHRIST

When Jesus tells His followers in the New Testament era that they will "inherit the land" when they are meek, they know exactly what

He is talking about. The history of the Old Testament and those who went before them was always kept fresh in their minds. These verses found in Psalm 37 are just some of the many references to the Israelites' inheriting the earth according to God's promises, when they chose to live in accordance with His will. This was the "promised land" that God had said He would take them to. He had allotted a portion for those who were meek, gentle, and willing to submit to His legitimate authority.

The main reason the first generation of Israelites who had been set free from captivity in Egypt did not make it to the promised land was their refusal to be meek. They would not submit to the legitimate authority of God—or the legitimate authority of Moses, whom God had appointed their leader. The Israelites' refusal to surrender to righteous authority canceled their ability to enter and enjoy the promises God had in store for them. The absence of this kingdom value known as gentleness cut them off from what Psalm 37 says is a land of promise.

Every believer reading this book has an allotted portion. This refers to the purpose and destiny God has determined to give you.

Ephesians 1:3 states that God, who is not bound by time or space, has already decided your blessings: "Blessed be the God and Father of our Lord Jesus Christ, who has blessed us with every spiritual blessing in the heavenly places in Christ."

God has already done everything He's ever going to do for you. I know it is hard to wrap your mind around that, but this passage reveals He has already "blessed us" with every potential blessing found in the spiritual realm. You don't have to say, "Lord, bless me." You've already been blessed. The problem is you may not always recognize or walk into the blessings set up for you because of your own lack of faith, hardness of heart, or sin.

God has placed on deposit a plethora of promises for you and me to inherit when we live according to His kingdom values. We know that one of these values is to live according to His revealed truth. This is the foundation. Resting on this foundation we find the important value of gentleness, or humility. When you and I live according to the principles of what it means to be meek, we will inherit the allotment God has for us.

Anyone who chooses to come under the control of Christ and His lordship will receive the promises He has prepared for them. Gentleness is like a key that unlocks the door of your destiny. When you live by this kingdom value, you will inherit the earth—you will get the promised land and gain access to what God has authorized you to have.

Many of us have been waiting for years for what God is already prepared to provide. Many have been praying for years for that which God could give them right now. But it is their own refusal to humbly live according to the precepts and principles of meekness that keeps them from accessing what they so desperately desire.

Far too often, the enemy is not external but within. A refusal to be meek will keep you from the full expression and experience of the spiritual provision of God in your life.

Let me describe it by comparing it to different banks. Say you bank at Commerce Bank. That's where you deposit your money so you can access it as you choose. Now, if you were to go to another bank, Guaranty Bank, and ask for your money, they would look at you funny and turn you away because you have not deposited anything there. You have gone to the wrong bank. And if you took a withdrawal slip from Guaranty Bank and presented it at your Commerce Bank, you would also be turned away. The reason is obvious—that withdrawal slip isn't authorized to work there.

Similarly, if you want a better marriage, a better career, more peace, or more joy—whatever it is spiritually that you are look-ing for—you must go to the right Source and ask Him to release your blessings. And you must present the correct withdrawal slip: a lifestyle based on His kingdom values.

I have a will. All four of my children are named in my will, which spells out who gets what should the time come for me to die. That's pretty standard. But I also have something that might not be standard in my will. It's a clause. The clause states that if any of my kids are acting the fool, they lose their inheritance. It's my will, so I make the standards.

Now, I don't mean if any of my kids are having difficulties or problems. That comes as part of life. I do mean, though, that if any of them adopts an ungodly, unrepentant lifestyle that is clearly evident to those around them, then they lose their inheritance. It's not that I don't love them. Actually, it is because I love them that this clause exists. Mainly because I wouldn't want to finance a lifestyle in which they would be wasting what God has given to them—a lifestyle of personal defeat. I wouldn't want the resources I left to them used on drug habits or to facilitate any other negative behavior. In other words, their inheritance is connected to their submission to God's rule in their lives.

> If you are living in alignment with God's kingdom values, then you get your allotted portion of spiritual blessings, provisions, and purpose. You don't have to fight for it. And you don't have to beg for it. It's yours when you humble yourself beneath Him according to His will and His way.

A lot of us have delayed our spiritual inheritance. We have cut ourselves out of the spiritual blessings already decreed for us by refusing to submit to the legitimate authority of God in our lives, as well as the legitimate authorities He places over us. If we could just see how much damage we are doing to ourselves with these lifestyle choices that countermand God's rightful place in our lives, we might think twice. And I'm not talking just about the obvious ones. There are many kingdom virtues, such as integrity, excellence, joy, kindness, and service, that we gloss over as unimportant in today's culture. And it is showing up in un-Christlike words and behavior toward others.

The good news is that if you are living in alignment with God's kingdom values, then you get your allotted portion of spiritual blessings, provisions, and purpose. You don't have to fight for it. You don't have to maneuver, politic, manipulate, or push people around for it. And you don't have to beg for it. It's yours when you humble yourself beneath Him according to His will and His way. Jesus said, "Blessed are the gentle, for they shall inherit the earth" (Matthew 5:5).

The psalmist writes in Psalm 73 that we are not to be envious of the wicked when we see them prospering. It's easy to envy, though, especially when you see evil people seemingly not only getting away with what they are doing but also benefiting from it. But the psalmist reminds us that the tables will turn. He writes in verses 17–20 about their fateful end,

> Then I perceived their end.
> Surely You set them in slippery places;
> You cast them down to destruction.
> How they are destroyed in a moment!
> They are utterly swept away by sudden terrors!
> Like a dream when one awakes,
> O Lord, when aroused, You will despise their form.

It might seem that living with kingdom values gets you nowhere in this life. It might appear that those who throw morality out the window are the ones who are prospering. But never become envious of the wicked. Things are not always as they appear. In fact, God will often use the enemy to set up and store riches for the righteous; He will take their profit and transfer it to the righteous in due time (Proverbs 13:22).

That's why Scripture urges us to seek first the kingdom of God (Matthew 6:33). When we seek God's kingdom and His agenda to be made manifest in our lives first and foremost, He tells us that "all these things will be added to you."

One of the most exciting things in life is to watch God work stuff out for you when you didn't have any idea how it could possibly be done. There's nothing quite like it. But that is not an experience everyone gets to have, because it belongs to the meek, the gentle. It belongs to those who humble themselves under God and align their lives under His rule. It is reserved for those who are committed to Christ and the will of God.

God has an allotment for you. And while circumstances in your life might have delayed your receiving it, there are things you can do right now to usher in His blessings and favor. He has a spiritual inheritance for you to experience right now, but not if you live in spiritual rebellion. Living contrary to the expressions of kingdom virtues in your life is living in a spirit of rebellion. God has created and called you to express His image to a world in need. You do that by modeling His heart to others.

Moses is a great example of meekness. He is called the meekest man on earth in Numbers 12:3. Keep in mind that meek is not weak. This is the man who stood before Pharaoh and commanded him to "let my people go." It is the same man who lifted his rod so that the Red Sea would be opened up and people could cross through. Moses wasn't weak. He was meek.

He was willing to step up and help others out, but he also knew that when it came to his own battles, God would fight for him, as He did with David facing Goliath. We see an example of this when Moses' siblings, Miriam and Aaron, became upset with him because he married a Cushite. His marriage to the Cushite woman stirred up conflict in the home for a couple of reasons. One was that it was an interracial marriage, and Miriam and Aaron didn't approve. Another was that Moses' wife would now carry more influence over him than Miriam did, so there was a battle for influence.

Moses knew his family was upset with him because they not only told him, they also told everyone around them (Numbers 12:1–2). They confronted him, and they confronted others about him. In today's terminology, they threw Moses under the bus. But rather than duke it out in a family debate involving shouting, cussing, and fussing, Moses knew to go to God instead. We see that in verse 3, which says, "Now the man Moses was very humble, more than any man who was on the face of the earth." We read nothing of Moses' response other than that he was humble.

What happens next is what happens when you trust God for your defense. We read that God called all three of them to Him in order to confront them. A few verses later we read what happened, "So the anger of the LORD burned against them and He departed. But when the cloud had withdrawn from over the tent, behold, Miriam was leprous, as white as snow. As Aaron turned toward Miriam, behold, she was leprous" (vv. 9–10). Aaron acknowledged the foolishness of what they had done and went on to ask Moses to forgive them and not hold it against them.

Meek people may fight for other people—to defend, deliver, or assist them, but they don't have to fight for themselves. God does that. You'll remember that Jesus became so upset with what the money changers were doing in the temple that He overturned the tables. He fought for those being taken advantage of by the greedy group in control. Yet when He hung on the cross, He looked only to God. He didn't open His mouth. He had entrusted himself to the Father, who rules over all. As we see later, He was raised from the dead—overcoming the enemy's plan to defeat Him.

Living with the kingdom value of gentleness or meekness invites God into the equation. It invites God to enact His justice in the situation. But you only get to see God intervene if you are meek. When you submit yourself to the legitimate authority that God has assigned to you, God shows up when you need Him most.

It's been a while now, but there was a time when I got stranded alongside the road. My car had broken down as I was on my way to a speaking engagement south of Dallas. So I called AAA. In a very short time, a representative from AAA showed up. They hooked my car to their tow truck with a harness and lifted it up. I then got in the truck to ride with the driver as he towed my car to the station to get it repaired.

My car wouldn't have been repaired and I would have remained stranded if I hadn't been willing to yield to the harness of the one sent to help me. Insisting on my own way would have gotten me nowhere. Living with the kingdom value of gentleness allows you to recognize that you don't always know the best thing to do. Nor do you always have access to that which can deliver you. But if you will allow yourself to be harnessed—the Bible calls it "yoked"—with Jesus Christ, He will make your load light and your burden easy. He will help you get where you need to go so that you do not wind up stranded on this highway called life.

10

HUNGRY FOR RIGHTEOUSNESS

One of the issues that determines the outcome of any sporting competition, and especially football, is hunger. Hunger often decides the result. How hungry is each team for a victory? How badly do they want it? The role of hunger is why you will rarely see back-to-back repeats of Super Bowl champions because often when a victory of that magnitude is achieved, the hunger to go get it again diminishes.

Hunger dictates actions. Actions produce outcomes. Without hunger, an athlete can become lazy. He or she can skimp on their drills or cheat on their reps. Without hunger, an athlete can lose focus. The glitz and the glam and the dollars that come with a past success often do more to harm an athlete's or team's future success than any opponent ever could do.

Hunger helps motivate a person to push harder, dig deeper, and pursue their goal with more passion. Hunger helps you win.

That's why, when we get to the next kingdom value in Jesus' Sermon on the Mount, we shouldn't be surprised that he uses a familiar phrase. In trying to create a correlation we could understand quickly, Jesus said we are blessed when we are hungry and thirsty. Now, He didn't mean when we hunger and thirst for food and drink. Rather, He said, "Blessed are those who hunger and thirst for righteousness, for they shall be satisfied" (Matthew 5:6).

Those who live with the kingdom value of desire for God's ways, His rules, and His righteous standards will experience satisfaction.

Appetite is one of the great indicators to a doctor of your health. A consistently poor appetite is an indication of a deeper problem. That's why one of the first questions a nurse or a doctor will ask when you go in for a visit is how your appetite has been. Similarly, spiritual appetite is one of the great indicators to God of your spiritual health. If you experience no appetite for Him and His truth or values, then you are revealing a lack of need for and connection to Him. This particular kingdom value is easy to spot. The idiom "hunger and thirst" shows up as a passionate desire propelled by heavy longing. It produces actions that are recognizable.

We live in a day when most of us don't have to worry about being hungry for very long. Access to food in the Western world is replete. Sure, we might be inconvenienced by the time it takes to go to a store or restaurant, but very few of us in our nation know true physical hunger.

It wasn't like that in biblical days, when there were no freezers or refrigerators. People had to hustle for food day in and day out because it couldn't typically be preserved for extended periods. In addition, food preparation was often laborious and lengthy. People didn't necessarily snack all day like so many have become accustomed to doing today. They couldn't just wake up in the middle of the night and go to the refrigerator or pantry for a quick snack. Meals had designated times. Leftovers didn't last long. Due to consumption, rot, the need to feed livestock, or some other reason, there wasn't much in the way of leftovers. Little is wasted when little is all you've got. Many who lived when Jesus spoke these words knew exactly what it was to be hungry. They knew what it was to be thirsty. They knew what it was like to have gone an extended amount of time without the nourishment they needed.

Real hunger can be so deep and so gnawing that it literally hurts, keeping the sufferer awake all night. This is the hunger and the thirst Jesus spoke about. He told us in this kingdom value that we are blessed if we have this kind of hunger and thirst for righteousness. We are blessed when we passionately desire righteousness and eagerly pursue it—when we truly know our need for righteousness and take the necessary actions to feed it. That's the hunger and the thirst Jesus spoke about. It is the same hunger and thirst referenced frequently in Scripture. Multiple times we read of this hunger:

- ► "My soul is crushed with longing after Your ordinances at all times" (Psalm 119:20).
- ► "As the deer pants for the water brooks, so my soul pants for You, O God" (Psalm 42:1).
- ► "O God, You are my God; I shall seek You earnestly; my soul thirsts for You, my flesh yearns for You, in a dry and weary land where there is no water" (Psalm 63:1).
- ► "Indeed, while following the way of Your judgments, O LORD, we have waited for You eagerly; Your name, even Your memory, is the desire of our souls. At night my soul longs for You, indeed, my spirit within me seeks You diligently; for when the earth experiences Your judgments the inhabitants of the world learn righteousness" (Isaiah 26:8–9).
- ► "That I may know Him and the power of His resurrection and the fellowship of His sufferings, being conformed to His death" (Philippians 3:10).
- ► "Like newborn babies, long for the pure milk of the word, so that by it you may grow in respect to salvation" (1 Peter 2:2).
- ► "He humbled you and let you be hungry, and fed you with manna which you did not know, nor did your fathers know,

that He might make you understand that man does not live by bread alone, but man lives by everything that proceeds out of the mouth of the LORD" (Deuteronomy 8:3).

As in these Scriptures, there exists one common trait that shows up among the great people of Scripture, and that is their hunger and thirst after God. They are passionate in their pursuit of God. They are on fire to find Him and to experience Him at a deeper level. The longing cry of their hearts echoes Moses' "show me Your glory" (Exodus 33:18).

One of the reasons so many of us experience so little of God is that we are not hungry. Hungry people are going to do everything in their power to locate some food. They are going to think of little else. Hungry and thirsty people are going to remove distractions and cut short diversions so they can find something to eat or drink. They are desperate for something that will satisfy. They need it. They long for it.

One of the ways I often travel when I'm on the East Coast is by train, particularly if I am traveling between major cities. I just get on a train and in a few hours or less I am at my destination. If you've ridden a train, you probably have noticed that the cost of food is higher than the cost of food elsewhere. On a train they will charge you an unconscionable amount—as much as $10 for a hot dog or $8 for a soda. You might even pay $5 just for a small bag of chips.

They have chosen to charge you so much on the train because they know you can't go anywhere else—you have no other options. No one is going to hop off the train to grab a meal and then hop back on. Theirs is the only gig in town, so they price themselves like the only gig in town.

Sure, passengers might say they simply won't pay that much on a train and they won't support such an extortion-based business model. But that really depends on how hungry they are, or how hungry they get as the train keeps moving on. Because if they get hungry enough, neither the price tag nor their principles will prohibit them from pursuing the food they want.

When my siblings and I complained about something my mom was cooking and we didn't want to eat it, she used to tell us that we just weren't hungry enough. We would excuse ourselves from the table and head elsewhere in the house, only to hear her say, "You'll be back. When you get hungry enough, it'll be here." This is because my mom knew, as many moms do, that people who are truly hungry aren't that picky. They need food, and they won't let their preferences keep them from getting the nutrition and sustenance that will satisfy their bodies' needs.

Most Christians only want to nibble on spiritual food. It used to be that Sunday sermons might be an entire meal, which a lot of Christians would try to survive on for the rest of the week. But these days, with so much of Sunday worship centered more on celebrities preaching or singing, you don't even get a full meal. You might get a few bites here or there, but it's an appetizer at best. Now, a Sunday meal would never get anyone through an entire week anyhow, let alone a Sunday appetizer. If someone tried to live like that in the physical realm, they might be dead by the next Sunday. Nourishment requires consistency.

When Jesus speaks of our kingdom value involving a passionate pursuit of righteousness, He is indicating an ongoing priority. He is not talking about a verse a day that keeps the devil away. Or popping open a Bible app and scanning a few passages. Or listening to a podcast for a few minutes as you drive. If that's how a hungry person pursued food, that person would be malnourished in no time. When Jesus speaks of those who hunger and thirst for righteousness, He means people who remove the distractions and excesses in life that are not contributing to their pursuit of God. They don't browse multiple menus. They look to and long for God.

In the same way our physical bodies need food to survive, our souls need righteousness to survive. Righteousness is not something nice to add on the side; it is a necessity for life. We all understand

> When Jesus speaks of those who hunger and thirst for righteousness, He means people who remove the distractions and excesses in life that are not contributing to their pursuit of God. They don't browse multiple menus. They look to and long for God.

that if you go long enough without food or water, you will die. The body is designed to work with the fuel of food and water. The body demands it.

Similarly, spiritual life demands righteousness to function as it was designed to function. The Bible calls the spiritual being the "divine nature" (2 Peter 1:4). Righteousness is the nutrient God provides for your divine nature.

This righteousness isn't an ethereal term referring to some intangible halo hovering over certain people. Righteousness is very real. It involves making choices on a regular basis that promote your living in accordance with God's will. It can be described as right living. It includes identifying God's will on a matter and seeking to line up your life in accordance with that. To put it simply, it means aligning under God's kingdom rule.

Problems arise when people search for the wrong food to feed a legitimate spiritual need for righteousness. Isaiah 55:2 says,

> Why do you spend money for what is not bread, and your wages for what does not satisfy? Listen carefully to Me, and eat what is good, and delight yourself in abundance.

Enjoying cake is one thing. Seeking to satisfy the needs of the body with cake is another. Most of us understand that. But when it comes to spiritual nourishment, that truth gets lost. Far too many believers today seek for that which "is not bread," and they waste their money on that which "does not satisfy." Only a deceived person would believe that eating cake every day as your only source of food would provide what the body is calling for. Likewise, only a deceived person would believe that spiritual well-being is sustained by listening to a sermon once a week, or reading a few verses of the Bible and saying a prayer before they eat.

Cake is fundamentally empty calories. While it may give you a semblance of satisfaction for a short time, it will not provide lasting nutrition. Cake is not designed to nourish the cellular structure of the body. It might be enjoyable, but it does not satisfy long-term. It does not have staying power. In fact, a lot of people become even more hungry after eating cake because the sugar and carbs stimulate the brain to crave more food. Thus, it starts a cycle of feeding that is sometimes difficult to stop. When you and I try to nourish our divine nature with that which is not bread and that which does not satisfy, we wind up starving to spiritual death, all the while craving more of the world's ways.

MAKING THE MOST OF WHAT YOU'VE GOT

Within our new nature, God has placed righteousness. The Bible calls it "imputed" righteousness (Romans 4:24 KJV). This transaction occurred when you accepted Jesus Christ as your personal sin bearer. At that moment, God took your sin and charged it to Jesus. Jesus never committed a sin himself, but the sins of we who are in the world were charged to His account.

At the same time that God charged Jesus' account with your sin at salvation, He also took the righteousness of Christ and credited your account with it. Thus, you are perfectly righteous on credit. Righteousness is the new divine nature.

Philippians 2:12–13 tells us what we are called to do with the righteous divine nature credited to us through the perfection of Jesus Christ. It says,

So then, my beloved, just as you have always obeyed, not as in my presence only, but now much more in my absence, work out your salvation with fear and trembling; for it is God who is at work in you, both to will and to work for His good pleasure.

The concept from this passage is that while God provides righteousness through our salvation, we have a participatory role in accessing the righteousness in our account. Acting out that righteousness is what satisfies the hunger and the thirst of the spiritual being. Without the execution of the righteousness that has been planted within us, the soul starves.

Despite the fact that you may go to church or engage in religious activities, if you are not hungering and thirsting after what your soul truly needs, you will starve spiritually. In order for your soul to flourish, it requires a consistent feeding of righteousness. The soul is nourished when you align yourself in accordance with the truth of God.

For example, if you drive a car that requires unleaded fuel but opt to fill it up with diesel instead, you will be in for a rough ride and you won't get very far. You will simply sputter down the road until you stop. It doesn't matter how new or expensive your car is. If you put diesel fuel in a car that's designed for unleaded, you'll ruin it.

You have to put unleaded fuel into a car designed to run on unleaded fuel. That's not too difficult for most of us to comprehend. And yet when we put all of the world's junk and all the culture's chaotic stuff into our souls, we wonder why we can only sputter through life.

We can't make it on the world's fuel because our divine nature requires righteousness based on truth. We run smoothly when we align our thoughts, decisions, and words under the overarching rule of God in our life. Doing anything else will cause problems under the hood of our souls.

From time to time when I am scheduled to preach, I'll look out into the congregation during a song or some other part of the service. Without fail, I'll see a mother with a baby in her arms, usually sitting toward the back so she can get to one of the cry rooms if the baby starts fussing. But normally the mother will try to console the baby first with a pacifier. The problem comes when the baby realizes that the pacifier is fake food. It's a piece of rubber designed to trick a kid. No matter how much the baby sucks on the pacifier, the baby won't be receiving any nourishment.

After a while, the baby will let out a loud cry at being fooled and frustrated. If the baby could talk, you might hear something like "Mama, you're playing with my emotions!" That's when the mom will get up and go to the cry room to feed the baby. A baby can only be pacified with fake food for so long. If the hunger is strong enough, the entire congregation will hear the cry.

Many people come to church on Sunday and are satisfied with a pacifier sermon or a pacifier song that makes them feel good for a moment. But not too long after the sermon or the song, they will discover they are still hungry. The feeding of the soul demands a consistency in righteousness, or it will go hungry. And when your soul is hungry, your whole life cries out in chaos. When we have enough souls who are hungry or starving, our whole culture cries out in chaos.

Jesus said that you are blessed when you hunger and thirst for the only thing the soul can digest. When you align your life in accordance with the truth of God, you will be feeding yourself with righteousness. Nothing else you give the soul will satisfy it. No matter how often you try to feed your soul with other things, it will never be satisfied with anything else.

To be satisfied is to be at rest, to feel at peace. It is to have a settled sensation within you that allows you to live in the moment rather than be mired in the past or worried about the future. Jesus calls it the abundant life and tells us in John 10:10 that it is this abundant life that He came to give us the opportunity to experience and enjoy. The psalmist describes it this way:

▶ "The young lions do lack and suffer hunger; but they who seek the LORD shall not be in want of any good thing" (Psalm 34:10).

▶ "For He has satisfied the thirsty soul, and the hungry soul He has filled with what is good" (Psalm 107:9).

To be satisfied is to lack nothing. Now, that doesn't mean you won't lack some things on your wish list. To be satisfied is to know that you are well provided for—your needs have all been met. You will be able to live a contented life.

If you are living an unsatisfied life where you run from one relationship to the next, or one church to the next, or one hobby, vacation, career, or ideology to the next—you need to check what kind of food you are eating. If you are relying on the world, the culture, the political pundits, or the talk-show hosts to satisfy you, you will starve. But if you are choosing to focus on the truth of God, His kingdom, and how to live your life under His rule, you will enjoy a sense of well-being.

God will remove the discontentment when you pursue His will and good pleasure. He will remove the misery that you thought was related to your circumstances but was really related to your lack of a divine perspective.

God will meet your every need like a shepherd who cares for his flock if you will look to Him as the source of your satisfaction. He will give you the wisdom you need to make better choices so you don't have to keep reliving the same terrible lessons again and again. He will give you the self-control you need to not open your mouth and join the division and hatred so prevalent in our culture today. He will give you the courage that is required to live in a world where the only consistent reality is that nothing is consistent at all.

If you find yourself going through the motions, and either nothing makes you happy or you have to conjure up happiness to distract you from your unhappiness, you are not pursuing righteousness. I can say that because Jesus promises in His Word that you will be satisfied when you are pursuing righteousness.

Satisfaction is yours for the taking. It's as simple as conforming your thoughts and your actions to the will of God. Much of the disenchantment and the despondency we face week after week or month after month is tied to famished souls. If the body of Christ would stop dining solely on spiritual doughnuts, as pleasant as they taste and as easy as they go down, we would be able to impact the chaos in our culture and transform it for the glory of God.

But we won't do that until we, as a collective body, are as passionate about the truth of God's Word and the primacy of His rule as we are about everything else we've placed ahead of Him. Until we reject illegitimate sources of nutrition and replace them with the truth, we will remain ineffective followers unable to make much of a difference at all.

If the physical body needs food several times a day just to function, how much more do you think the spiritual being needs righteousness on a regular basis? Our souls are starving because we have relegated our relationship with God and His rule to the status of a social media influencer trying to get us to buy the latest shoes or home goods.

> If the body of Christ would stop dining solely on spiritual doughnuts, as pleasant as they taste and as easy as they go down, we would be able to impact the chaos in our culture and transform it for the glory of God.

God doesn't just want to influence you, He—as God—is in charge. He is the ultimate Ruler, and He rules over all. To rightly align under Him, you will need to consistently feed your soul with righteous thoughts, righteous words, and righteous behavior.

And if you're not used to feeding on so much righteousness at one time, then start where you can. Set down your cellphone and pick up your Bible. Turn off the television and read a book or listen to a podcast on righteousness-based principles. Start where you are, and as you continue, you will notice your hunger increasing each day. What used to be five minutes of reading will turn into twenty.

As your soul expands with the righteousness of God, your hunger and your thirst will increase to meet the growing appetite of your soul. I encourage you to make this kingdom value of hungering and thirsting after righteousness—intentionally pursuing God and His truth—part of your everyday life. As you do, you will discover what it means to be truly satisfied.

11

MERCIFUL

The kingdom values Jesus taught on in the Sermon on the Mount lay out the road to spiritual blessing. As we've seen, it starts with being poor in spirit. This is when you recognize your own spiritual bankruptcy and you declare your lack of capacity to satisfy your own spiritual needs independently of God. The people who choose to live in this awareness get the kingdom. They gain access to the King of the kingdom and all that entails.

Next, we looked at mourning over our sin. This should come naturally to those who are poor in spirit because recognizing your own spiritual inadequacy leads to sorrow of the soul over breaching God's standards. God lets us know that when we arrive at this place in developing our personal kingdom values, we are setting ourselves up to receive His comfort.

Building upon these first two, we come to the kingdom value of gentleness. As a reminder, gentleness is not weakness; it is power under control. When you submit to divine authority, you become one who experiences the inheritances of the kingdom. You gain access to that which has been ordained for you both in this life on earth and in eternity.

This is a natural progression of kingdom values.

As you partake of more and more of the benefits and blessings of the kingdom, your hunger for the King's values will increase. This shows up as a desire and thirst for righteousness. The more you come to know of God's satisfying abilities in your own life, the more spiritual drive will rise up within you. You will live with a greater passion to discover that which pleases God.

After these first four kingdom values, which center primarily on the internal self, Jesus turns to one that deals with extending care and compassion to others. He says, "Blessed are the merciful, for they shall receive mercy." To understand what it means to live with this value of being merciful, we need to first understand mercy.

Mercy assumes that there is a miserable situation needing relief. Mercy can only show up when there have been circumstances to warrant it. Mercy can be defined as compassion for someone in need. It involves reducing, removing, or relieving someone's distress.

Scripture tells us that our salvation is the result of mercy. We read in Titus 3:5, "He saved us, not on the basis of deeds which we have done in righteousness, but according to His mercy, by the washing of regeneration and renewing by the Holy Spirit."

We also read in Ephesians 2:4–5, "But God, being rich in mercy, because of His great love with which He loved us, even when we were dead in our transgressions, made us alive together with Christ." In other words, God is rich in relieving people's pain, as well as removing or reducing the weight of distress, discouragement, brokenness, and problems that come our way.

In fact, mercy summarizes God's reaction to our individual misery (Psalm 130:1–8). It involves more than feeling sorry for someone. Anyone can feel sorry for someone but still do nothing to help. Mercy means the sorrow you feel for someone shows up in your actions to help relieve their pain. Mercy always involves action to reduce or remove the misery that has come about in someone else's life.

The Bible reminds us of God's abundant mercy toward each of us. We read of God's mercy in several places:

- ▶ "The Lord's loving kindnesses indeed never cease, for His compassions never fail. They are new every morning; great is Your faithfulness" (Lamentations 3:22–23).
- ▶ "For the LORD your God is a merciful God; he will not abandon or destroy you or forget the covenant with your ancestors, which he confirmed to them by oath" (Deuteronomy 4:31 NIV).
- ▶ "The LORD is good to all, and His mercies are over all His works" (Psalm 145:9).
- ▶ "Because of the tender mercy of our God, with which the Sunrise from on high will visit us" (Luke 1:78).

God's mercy serves as an example for how we are to be merciful to others. Mercy isn't contingent upon what someone else can do. It doesn't depend on whether the other person deserves it. If we needed to earn the air we breathe or the sunrise that gives us light, which God so mercifully supplies, none of us would be here. Mercy presupposes that the recipient is not entitled to what he or she is receiving.

Thus, when you show someone mercy, it's not a favor. It's not a business transaction. It's not quid pro quo. Mercy provides relief from sorrow and pronounces a state of well-being on the recipient, regardless of what they have done up to that point.

There are two common reasons people need mercy. One is due to the debilitating impact of sin in their lives. The other is due to the painful weight of circumstances that have arisen that are not the result of their own actions. Regardless of the cause of the suffering, mercy extends relief to those who need it.

As our nation has become more polarized on the topics of politics, race, and health, I have witnessed an increased lack of mercy between the two sides. There are those on the vaccinated side of the COVID-19 battle who argue that medical care and insurance should be withheld from those who are unvaccinated. While this argument might seem sound to those making it, logic precludes us from applying it to all things. For example, would medical care and insurance then be withheld from those who smoke? Or for those with a BMI over thirty? Or for those who participate in extreme sports? I could go on with examples, but you get the point.

What has struck me even more, on social media at least, is that there seems to be an increasing number of people who applaud the deaths of those of another political or medical viewpoint. Our culture has fallen into an abyss of vitriol and hatred on every level. And unfortunately, the church has participated more often than we would like to admit.

Mercy is sorely lacking today—whether in our words or in our actions. Yet Jesus says it is this kingdom value that sets up the boomerang effect in your life to receive it back. People who show mercy can expect to receive mercy. This kingdom value brings into clear view the biblical command to do unto others as you would have them do to you (Matthew 7:12). The more mercy you are willing to show to others, the more access you have to mercy for yourself. And who couldn't use a bit of mercy from time to time? I think we all can.

> People who show mercy can expect to receive mercy. This kingdom value brings into clearer view the biblical command to do unto others as you would have them do to you.

Showing mercy to others requires that we first adopt the previous kingdom values in our lives, because mercy must be pure in motive for it to be mercy. A prideful person will never show mercy. The act of mercy is birthed in humility. Jesus gives us an example in Luke 18:10–14 of two men with very different levels of mercy. One man was a Pharisee, and the other man was a publican, also known as a tax collector. We read,

"Two men went up into the temple to pray, one a Pharisee and the other a tax collector. The Pharisee stood and was praying this to

144

himself: 'God, I thank You that I am not like other people: swindlers, unjust, adulterers, or even like this tax collector. I fast twice a week; I pay tithes of all that I get.' But the tax collector, standing some distance away, was even unwilling to lift up his eyes to heaven, but was beating his breast, saying, 'God, be merciful to me, the sinner!' I tell you, this man went to his house justified rather than the other; for everyone who exalts himself will be humbled, but he who humbles himself will be exalted."

The Pharisee was confident he was doing all the right things. His heart was rooted in pride. But the publican knew he needed help. He knew he made mistakes and committed sins. Jesus made it clear to us through this parable that the one who asked for mercy out of a heart of humility received the mercy he needed. Jesus also emphasized that the Pharisee who had exalted himself would at some point be humbled. He would find himself in a position where he realized he needed mercy. But by then, without a change of heart, it would be too late to access it.

Similarly, when you and I go through our lives with a heart of pride and refuse to address the sins that are creating the misery and chaos that consume us, we will neither show others mercy nor receive any for ourselves. Yet we can rest assured that there will come a day when we will know how much we need it.

When you call out to God for mercy, keep in mind that your previous actions will affect how He responds to you. Do not blame God if He withholds the mercy you feel you need. You might want to review your history and see whether you showed mercy to others in their times of need.

You can always request mercy, but you can never demand it. And while God is rich in mercy, as we saw in the Scriptures earlier in this chapter, He decides how much to give predicated on what you have done to others.

This isn't a secret hidden in His Word. It should come as no surprise, because God has outlined for us in several locations that how we treat others will impact how He treats us. To skip the application of this kingdom value in your own life and to adopt the cultural norm of criticism, judgment, blame, and even mocking of those in need with whom you disagree is to set up a roadblock to your own access to mercy. Yes, maybe their decisions did lead to a difficult outcome, and they are living with the consequences of their own wrong choices. But there are times in all of our lives when that is true.

To fail to show someone mercy simply because they may have either caused or contributed to the pain they are experiencing is a dangerous stance to take. When you do, you can be assured that when it comes time for you to need mercy from the consequences of your own wrong choices, God will remember how you treated others.

Now, there is a second reason that people need mercy. That's when circumstances outside of their control have caused chaos in their lives. Perhaps a person was born handicapped in some way. It could be that a weather catastrophe occurred in their region. Maybe they are suffering from cutbacks at work, or an accident on the job or on the road. There are countless reasons people are miserable through no fault of their own. We've all experienced these times. It is during these seasons or situations when we need someone to intervene and lift the burden that we discover how refreshing mercy truly can be.

It is also in these times that God looks at our track record of showing—or not showing—mercy to those in need. We will be blessed with God's mercy if we have been merciful to others. Granted, being merciful runs contrary to the dog-eat-dog society we live in. But it is a kingdom value we should live out—one that will come back to bite us if we fail to apply it regularly to others.

Now, I understand, you can't help everyone. No one can. But to live with this kingdom value of mercy means that you make an effort to remove the burden and lessen the misery for those you can. You might not be able to be merciful to everybody, but you can be merciful to somebody on a regular basis. You can make showing mercy a lifestyle and not an event.

It starts with altering your viewpoint to one that is rooted in humility. Once you do that, you will begin to judge less and help more. Mercy is a natural outgrowth of kingdom living. If you focus on adopting the first four kingdom values, you'll soon discover that this fifth one comes naturally to you.

MERCY IN ACTION

My son Anthony had been sponsoring a child in Africa for a number of years when he was invited to fly out and see him. They had never seen each other, even though Anthony had been sending money for food and school for some time. Anthony jumped at the opportunity and took the nearly day-long flight to Africa and the lengthy drive into the interior village where the boy he sponsored lived.

One of the interesting things Anthony shared with us when he returned is that the little boy he sponsored had been given a name that when translated into English means "to forget." The reason they chose this name was because his region had been decimated by AIDS. So the child had been given a name to help put the past behind him and look forward to the future. The mercy he had received up to that point enabled him to forget a lot of the misery he had been born into.

What's more, when Anthony met with the young boy's father, he asked him what his dream was. His father told him he dreamed of a home for his family where when it rained, the roof kept the water out. At that time, they had a grass roof and it always leaked during the rainy season. When Anthony asked him how much it cost, he told him the equivalent of around three hundred dollars.

Now, Anthony could have said he would pray for him that God would provide. Or he could have wished him all the best with his dream. He could have even felt sorry for him. But none of that would be considered mercy. Instead, Anthony sent the family the three hundred dollars necessary to build a substantial roof that would keep out the rain.

God is able to meet the needs of those who look to Him. But what we often forget is that He frequently chooses to do that through each of us. That's what mercy is all about. If you and I are content to spew phrases of encouragement toward each other that Jesus is the Rose of Sharon and Balm in Gilead as well as the Bright and Morning Star but we refuse to turn the light on when someone is lost in the darkness, we are no different from the Pharisees. We are no different from those who think their own righteousness will save them in their hour of need.

You'll probably never come across anyone more able to comfort someone else than a person who has just passed through a season of grief. Similarly, you'll probably never come across someone who is more willing to help another person financially than someone who has just passed through a season of financial strain. This can be applied to any number of scenarios, because when you and I pass through the waters of the weight and strain of the world and we find out how important mercy is, we are more willing to offer it to others.

Yet with this kingdom value, God is asking you to step out in faith and show mercy to others *first*, because of the mercy He has shown you through salvation and His daily provisions. He is asking you to be the Good Samaritan, and not just tell the story to your kids or teach it in Sunday school. God is asking you and me—all of us as His body—to be the hands and feet of Jesus, sharing His mercy through us to others.

You will be blessed when you show mercy to others. You will be blessed when you are inconvenienced for others and take their needs into account as you make your decisions for the day. You will be blessed when you consider those less fortunate than you. You will be blessed when you share the love of Jesus by giving others the value and dignity they so desperately need. After all, there is coming a day when you are going to need relief, when you are going to need help in forgetting the pain you've gone through. There is coming a day when you are going to need someone to reach down and lift you up, or help remove the weight that has collected on your shoulders.

When that day comes and you call on God for mercy, He is going to check your own mercy record and see how easily you showed mercy to others He placed along your path. Friend, if you want God to relieve your burdens and lighten your load, you need to stop skipping over the opportunities He gives you to do the same for others. What goes around really does come around when it has to do with kingdom values.

> God is asking you to step out in faith and show mercy to others *first*, because of the mercy He has shown you through salvation and His daily provisions. He is asking you to be the Good Samaritan, and not just tell the story to your kids.

Have you ever been on a customer service line and been told that the call is being recorded for quality assurance? The business managers do that so they can go back and check that their customer service agents are operating according to the standards they have established. Likewise, when you call on God for mercy, He has established some kingdom values standards that He is monitoring. It might be a selfish way of looking at why you should show mercy, but this is how Jesus framed it. He made it clear that those who show mercy will be shown mercy. Or, to reverse that, those who do not show mercy run the risk of not being shown mercy when they need it.

Of course, God can go outside of His prescribed plans any time He wants to do so. He can show mercy to whomever He wants to at any time He wants to. But what Jesus is stressing in this kingdom value is that there exists a boomerang effect when you show mercy. Or another way to state it in today's language is that there is an incentive to showing mercy. The more you give, the more you set yourself up to receive. What's more, you can feel confident in asking God to show you mercy when you have a history of showing it to others.

Nehemiah is a perfect example of this in the Bible. He had a comfortable position in a comfortable location with a comfortable outlook on life. After all, He was the cupbearer to the king. But despite his comfort, Nehemiah's heart became burdened for his people, the Israelites. His heart became broken over the plight of Jerusalem.

So all throughout the book named after him in Scripture, we see Nehemiah leaving the comfort of his surroundings and going out to help people who are hurting. He leads the campaign to rebuild the city. He brings justice to a group of people who were being treated unjustly. He feeds and clothes people in need, and he supplies and enables them to defend themselves, their families, and the city.

Yet as you read through the struggles and difficulties Nehemiah had to overcome in order to bring about such good for others, you see a repeated phrase. It's a short phrase, and you may have missed it if you read the chapters too quickly. But more than once you will find the phrase "Remember me, O my God, for good."

As Nehemiah is going about doing good for others and showing mercy to those in need, he is looking up to God in heaven and nudging Him with the phrase *remember me for good*. In other words, He is asking God to take note, to keep track. He's asking God to return the kindness to him when he needs it most. Nehemiah prays this way because Nehemiah knows the kingdom principle that giving sets you up to receive. That's what the Bible means when it says you are "more blessed to give than to receive" (Acts 20:35).

In Matthew 18:23–34, we see the opposite of Nehemiah's story. We read about a man who owed the king hundreds of thousands of dollars in today's currency. Knowing that he would go to debtors' prison because of what he owed, the man begged for mercy. The king showed him mercy and removed the debt. The problem came when the man returned home and ran across someone who owed him a lot less money. Rather than extend the same mercy he just received, he had the man thrown in prison for failing to pay him.

When the king heard what the man had done despite having been shown mercy for his own debt, he changed his earlier decision and revoked the man's freedom. As a result, he wound up in debtors' prison as well. James 2:13 summarizes the principle in that story when it says, "For judgment will be merciless to one who has shown no mercy; mercy triumphs over judgment."

This kingdom value still applies today. If you live your life so full of your goals, your dreams, your desires, and your wants that you skip over everybody else even though you are in a position to help them, you will be setting yourself up for failure. On the day you cry out for mercy, there will be none for you because you will have stored up none through your actions. By adopting and applying this kingdom value as a normal function of your everyday life, you will be positioning yourself for mercy.

Mercy is a powerful thing. Mercy enables you to join the heart of God in helping others. This then frees God's heart to help you. Mercy is one of life's most strategic actions. It sets you up to pray, *God, remember me for good* during your worst moments in life.

Let mercy be the outgrowth of a life rooted in an awareness of spiritual inadequacy, mourning, gentleness, and hunger for righteousness. When you do, you will discover the peace that comes from knowing that God will work everything out according to His great mercy.

12

PURE IN HEART

Many of you reading this book might struggle with allergies. Allergies tend to flare up when the dust and pollen in the air make it miserable to breathe. Stuffy noses, runny eyes, and congestion result—all because the air is contaminated by allergens. I know that those who struggle with allergies hope for better days when the air is clearer and cleaner. They look forward to a fresh rain to clear the skies so that the allergens no longer impact their well-being.

The next kingdom value we are going to look at in Jesus' Sermon on the Mount relates to the prerequisite God longs to see in you. Jesus states this precursor to further blessing when He says, "Blessed are the pure in heart, for they shall see God."

In the same way we desire air to be free from pollutants, allergens, and irritants so that what we breathe is pure, God desires that our hearts be free from pollutants, irritants, and impurities as well. He seeks a follower whose heart is unmixed, undivided, and undiluted in his or her love for Him. And when He finds a follower who fits that description, He delivers a unique blessing in that He reveals himself to them on a whole other level.

In other words, many of us are not seeing God for ourselves because we are taking in that which has contaminated our spiritual systems. We are allowing in the pollutants of the culture, which results in watery, itchy spiritual eyes. Everyone knows that it is more difficult to see clearly when your eyes are watering and red. These cultural contaminants cloud our vision to such a degree that we no longer recognize or experience God's work, power, provision, transformation, deliverance, and victory firsthand. Sure, we may hear about these things from others, but when we look at our own lives, we cannot see God up close and personal there.

In order to see God this way, your heart must be pure, undefiled. Spiritually speaking, a pure heart means having singleness of devotion. It means to love all of God with all of you, not just with a portion of you for a time. Purity of heart means you are no longer disconnected from God by something you have allowed to defile your relationship with Him.

As we've seen in some of the other kingdom values, God and sin are irreconcilable. The two don't get along. I used the illustration of garbage in your home as a way to help you see how God feels about sin. You wouldn't want to live in a house with rotten garbage piled up all around you, and neither does God want to abide in the temples of our souls with rotten, sinful garbage piled up all around. In order to get rid of the trash in our homes, we take it out. Similarly, we must repent of sin and turn from it in order to be clean within and have a pure heart. God simply can't be comfortable where unrighteousness is allowed to express itself freely.

This description of being pure in heart has to do with not allowing the contaminants of sin to penetrate the heart so as to cause God to distance himself from intimacy with you. See, many Christians today carry on a long-distance relationship with God. If God were the sun and they were a planet, they would be more like Pluto than Mercury. They are a long way off. And because they are so far from the sun, they are cold like Pluto too. The further you are from God, the colder your heart grows, because He is the source of love, compassion, and light.

What Jesus reminds us of in this kingdom value is that if we are to see God at a more intimate level than the average person does, and if we are to experience God more deeply than we ever have before, then we must chase after the cleansing of our heart. We must pursue purity.

Don't misunderstand this. Jesus' concern is about purity—real purity. It's easy to camouflage ourselves so that we look a lot cleaner than we are. We can dust off some wrong desires or scrub away some sin for a season. It's easy to mask unrighteousness with a righteous look or by using seemingly righteous sayings. Jesus wasn't born yesterday. He can see right past our façade. That's why He called the Pharisees out as He did when He said, "Woe to you, scribes and Pharisees, hypocrites! For you clean the outside of the cup and of the dish, but inside they are full of robbery and self-indulgence" (Matthew 23:25).

> If we are to see God at a more intimate level than the average person does, and if we are to experience God more deeply than we ever have before, then we must chase after the cleansing of our heart. We must pursue purity.

In other words, Jesus told them He saw past their attire that made it look like they and God were running buddies. He didn't fall for their fancy words or inside jokes that made it seem like they were hanging out with God on the regular. No, Jesus told them they were nothing but "whitewashed tombs" that inside were "full of dead men's bones" (v. 27). A whitewashed tomb might appear clean on the outside, but once you open the lid or peer under the stones, you'll find nothing but stench, rot, and filth of all kinds.

God is not after a purity of look, or a purity of location, or even a purity of religious activity. None of that matters if the heart itself is impure—a heart far removed from God.

Many of us don't drink the tap water in our homes. Instead, we run the water through a filtering system to remove the impurities or toxins within. We do not want the invisible bacteria, chemicals, or other matter to harm our bodies. We want to drink that which is pure, undefiled, and healthy. In fact, many of us have gone so far as to put whole-house water filtration systems in place, at no small expense. Pure water is a source of life to our bodies while contaminated water is a source of disease and ailments.

The way we feel about our water is the way God feels about our hearts. He knows that the contaminants of sin and the pollutants of pride only harm people. He doesn't want to see our hearts impure—not only because it offends Him but also because He knows how it destroys us. It destroys our relationships and our thought processes, and it even damages our dreams and destinies. Just as impurities cloud the water so you can no longer see clearly through it, impurities also cloud our heart, impacting our spiritual vision. We can no longer see the pristine nature of who God is and what He has placed within us.

BEAT OF THE HEART

To understand what Jesus is urging us to do in living according to this kingdom value, we need to take a deeper look at the heart. We're all familiar with what a heart is from a physiological perspective, but what is the heart when referenced from a theological or spiritual standpoint? God often uses spiritual concepts that have a physical counterpart, which helps us understand the spiritual concept more completely. In these cases, we start with the physical realm to gain an understanding there, and then apply it to the spiritual realm. Thus, understanding the function and purpose of the physical heart will help us gain greater insight into God's desire for us to live with purity in our spiritual heart.

All of us have a heart. The heart is the centerpiece of life. It's the pump that keeps life going. A person can survive without a hand or a foot. A person can even survive with no ears or eyes. But no human can survive without a heart. No heart, no life. This is because the heart pumps the source of life, blood, throughout your body. As Scripture says, "the life of the flesh is in the blood" (Leviticus 17:11).

Oxygen is carried throughout your body in the blood. Thousands of times a day, blood flows through the arteries to deliver life-giving oxygen and nutrients. If the heart stops pumping, all life will cease and all organs will suffer failure.

The purpose of your physical heart is to cause life to show up in every other location of your body. If and when your arteries become clogged with the wrong stuff, such as plaque, it reduces the ability of the blood to flow through. This then causes the heart to work overtime in order to deliver the life nutrients and oxygen throughout the body. If the arteries become too clogged, a heart attack can occur. That is why when doctors assess the health of a person's heart, two of the things they look at are how it holds up under stress and how freely the blood flows.

When the heart is functioning as it should, you don't even think about it. It's just there, doing its job. It's only when something is not right that you focus on your heart because it is serving notice to the rest of your body that it needs immediate attention.

Inside each of us resides the source of our spiritual life as well. We call it our soul. The soul includes your personality. It's your personhood. Your soul is the you that lives forever. Your soul is made up of three fundamental components: emotions, intellect, and will. Your emotions are what are known as your feelings. Your intellect is composed of your thoughts and understanding. Your will is your capacity to make choices. As a human with a soul, you can feel, you can think, and you can make choices.

But just as the body has a pump that pumps life to the physical man, the soul has a pump that pumps life to the spiritual man. God has given the spiritual heart to the soul just as He gave the physical heart to the body. We can refer to this spiritual pump in many terms. It is the core of the inner man that pumps the life of God into your personality.

It pumps God's thinking and His perspective into your spiritual mind. It supplies God's emotions and His choices into your will. And as long as this core of your soul is free to pump the spiritual nutrients the soul needs to survive, the soul remains healthy. In fact, the Bible says that the soul can remain healthy even when the body is not. We read in 2 Corinthians 4:16, "Therefore we do not lose heart, but though our outer man is decaying, yet our inner man is being renewed day by day."

In other words, in God's economy, the older you get on the outside, the younger you should be getting on the inside. As your body ages, your personality and thoughts should stay vitally energetic and youthful. So if your soul is as old as your body, then you are suffering from a spiritual heart problem. It means that the life principles of the Spirit are not being pumped throughout your soul. Proverbs 4:23 says, "Watch over your heart with all diligence, for from it flow the springs of life."

Your spiritual life reflects the condition of your spiritual core. If there exists an interruption within its flow or a buildup of sinful plaque that keeps it from circulating life throughout your soul, your spiritual life will deteriorate. As your spiritual life deteriorates, it begins to show up in your emotions, your thoughts, and your choices.

When you came to Christ for salvation, you were given a spiritual heart transplant. But this new spiritual heart only works as it was designed to work. It only pumps what you need spiritually if you are putting heart-healthy things into your life. If you choose to put spiritually damaging things into your life on a regular basis, your spiritual heart will decay and suffer. It will not be able to provide you with the clarity of thought, the stability of emotion, or the strength of will to fully maximize your kingdom purpose. Rather, you will join the ranks of those whose lives resemble and reflect the chaos in our culture.

THE POWER OF SEEING GOD CLEARLY

When you live with a singleness of devotion toward God, you gain clarity in your thoughts, stability in your emotions, and strength of will to make wise choices. You access peace. You tap into productivity. You see God. The purer your heart, the clearer your view of God becomes.

For far too many believers today, God is merely an idea. He's a concept, a ritual, or an entity in a book. For those who do not, or cannot, see God due to the levels of spiritual impurities in their souls, God never becomes an experiential reality. They never understand what it means to know God intimately. They are forced to wander through a maze of spiritual warfare littered with mines placed by the enemy, yet they are able to use only their physical eyes. They have no access to the Guide. They cannot see how to maneuver through the myriad of potential messes and mistakes because they do not know how to see with spiritual eyes.

Seeing God clearly also means seeing everything else spiritually. God is Spirit. To know Him intimately is to know His heart, His perspective. It is to see life from His viewpoint and live with a kingdom orientation. When you can view your life through the lens of the Holy Spirit, you don't see the people and the problems the way you used to. You see more than the limited physical realm in front of you. When you are not connected to God in a way that allows you to see Him and see through spiritual eyes, all you see is what you see in the natural. And if all you see is what you see, you do not see all there is to be seen.

A lot of the misery we experience in life is because we are slaves to what we see. We assume that what we see is all there is because we do not have God's perspective. God can see so much more than we can. He can see what is behind, in front, and all around. He is not bound by the physical limitations that we are. He can see all aspects of all things.

To see God, when you live according to the kingdom value of a pure spiritual heart, is to see what God sees. It is to gain entrance into His eternal perspective. Seeing God means perceiving and sensing His reality. It gives you and me the opportunity to view our lives through spiritual eyes. It opens up windows all around us through which we can gain clarity. Elisha's servant was limited by physical eyesight when he looked out over the territory and only saw the approaching army; seeing God enables us to be like Elisha, who prayed that God would open the servant's eyes. With spiritual eyes, the servant saw the spiritual warriors lined up to protect and defend them. He did not need to hide or cower in fear. The enemy that appeared to be encroaching on him would be stopped, but he was only able to realize that when he saw with spiritual eyes (2 Kings 6:15–17).

How many battles have you gone out to fight that God had already planned to defend you from? How many battle scars have you needlessly obtained attempting to wage spiritual warfare with physical weapons? Seeing God because you live with this kingdom value of pureness of heart gives you the ability to see life spiritually. You can see His hand steering you away from danger. You can see His heart lovingly directing you toward your destiny. You can see the potential pitfalls on the path you've chosen so that you can avoid them rather than fall into them.

But not only does seeing God give you greater spiritual perspective for protection purposes, such vision also gives you greater spiritual productivity too. When Moses asked to see God, He reminded Moses that no man could see God's face and live (Exodus 33:20). But Moses persisted in his desire. He wanted to see God and His glory. So God hid Moses in the cleft of the rock, and He allowed him to see His back (Exodus 33:23). Moses was allowed to see the glow left behind after God passed by. Like the vapor trail from an airplane that has flown on ahead, Moses saw the trail of God's glory.

What's more, once Moses was able to see God in that way, he began to write. He became inspired to write. He picked up his pen and his notepad and wrote, "In the beginning God created the heavens and the earth. The earth was formless and void, and darkness was over the surface of the deep, and the Spirit of God was moving over the surface of the waters" (Genesis 1:1–2).

Moses didn't stop there either. He went on to write the first five books of the Bible, even though he wasn't alive when Genesis took place. This is because Moses had seen God. He could look back and see what God had done so that he would be inspired by the Spirit to record it.

When you see God, He shows you what He is up to. He pulls back the curtain and reveals the activity and purposes behind the veil. When you see God, He can even reveal to you why things happened to you in your past to get you to your present. He can show you what you need to do now in order to make a better tomorrow.

Seeing God isn't the same as staring at a piece of art on a wall. He is not just something to admire and praise. Seeing God allows you to see you. It allows you to see that you are a reflection of Him, made in His image. It enables you to see why you were created and what you have been brought here to do. Seeing God peels off the cataracts clouding your spiritual eyes and reveals the working and mysteries of the spiritual realm. With this insight you can then navigate your days and your nights with wisdom.

> Seeing God peels off the cataracts clouding your spiritual eyes and reveals the working and mysteries of the spiritual realm. With this insight you can then navigate your days and your nights with wisdom.

The psalmist reminds us that purity of heart enables God to hear us when we pray (Psalm 66:18). It opens the floodgates of His goodness (Psalm 73:1). The writer of Hebrews puts it like this: "Pursue peace with all men, and the sanctification without which no one will see the Lord" (Hebrews 12:14). The real experience of God working, moving, leading, and governing in your life and blessing it flows out of the abundance of a pure heart. It flows from the springs of a sanctified soul.

Life is too complicated and lies are too frequent to rely on your physical understanding, especially these days. It's hard to tell who is telling the truth anymore when you turn on the news, or go on social media, or listen to your friends or family. It's like the world has turned into one continuous game of telephone, where misinterpretation after misinterpretation is all we have left to go on.

In the chaos of our culture today, you do not want to live limited to what you can see physically. You do not want to have to depend solely on your five senses. Only God offers a way to see things from His unlimited vantage point. But to do so you must be pure of heart. You don't get to access this blessing when you have a soul contaminated with sin. One of the primary sources of sin entering our lives comes through our minds. If you can get your mind right, the rest will follow. James says,

> You lust and do not have; so you commit murder. You are envious and cannot obtain; so you fight and quarrel. You do not have because you do not ask. You ask and do not receive, because you ask with wrong motives, so that you may spend it on your pleasures. You adulteresses, do you not know that friendship with the world is hostility toward God? Therefore whoever wishes to be a friend of the world makes himself an enemy of God. Or do you think that the Scripture speaks to no purpose: "He jealously desires the Spirit which He has made to dwell in us"? But He gives a greater grace. Therefore it says, "GOD IS OPPOSED TO THE PROUD, BUT GIVES GRACE TO THE HUMBLE." Submit therefore to God. Resist the devil and he will flee from you. Draw near to God and He will draw near to you. Cleanse your hands, you sinners; and purify your hearts, you double-minded.
>
> James 4:2–8

The way to purify your heart is to get rid of your double-mindedness (see James 1:6–8). Being double-minded means you are thinking two

161

different ways at the same time. You are carrying the Bible in one hand and the world in another. In order for you to resist the devil, you need to position yourself so that God is not resisting you.

If and when you live with double-mindedness, God will resist you because you have elevated your thoughts above His. You have given in to pride, assuming that you know as much as the Creator of the universe knows. And the Bible tells us that "God is opposed to the proud." God will resist you when you live with double-mindedness. Not only will this keep you from seeing God and His perspective more clearly for yourself, but it will invite Him to actively oppose you based on your propensity toward pride.

The only way to resist the devil is through the authority of God. The devil may not have authority, but he does have power. And if you were to put his power, cunning, wit, and scheming up against yours, he would win. You cannot beat the devil on your own. It is through your attachment to God and His kingdom authority manifest in the blood of Jesus Christ that you will gain access to the upper hand. But you can only attach yourself to God in this way when you approach Him with purity of heart.

If you truly want to see God, you cannot be duplicitous about His rule. You can't honor His rule sometimes only to go and honor the devil's rule at other times. You can't go back and forth between them and still expect to be able to access God's authority when you need it. In order for God to be up close and personal in your life— for you to really see Him and experience His reality operating in your life—your heart must be pure, meaning unmixed and single-minded. For your heart to be pure, your mind must be focused on God's perspective alone (see Isaiah 26:3).

You can't have both God and the world, both God's way and your way. Just like you can't have both darkness and light at the same time. First John 1:5–7 explains this:

> This is the message we have heard from Him and announce to you, that God is Light, and in Him there is no darkness at all. If we say

that we have fellowship with Him and yet walk in the darkness, we lie and do not practice the truth; but if we walk in the Light as He Himself is in the Light, we have fellowship with one another, and the blood of Jesus His Son cleanses us from all sin.

Notice when Jesus cleanses us from all sin. It's when we are walking in the Light. Many people miss that. Or they misread that and misunderstand it. They think that if they are walking in the Light, then they don't have any sin. But that's not what it says. It says that when you are walking in the Light, God cleanses you of your sin. That's because sin can be located and exposed by the Light.

Let me explain. Have you ever gotten up in the middle of the night and tried to navigate through the dark to go use the restroom or go get a drink of water? Even if you know your way around, when you are in the dark you are going to miss something. For example, maybe you left a pair of shoes out in the middle of the floor. Or maybe the pet left a toy out. Or maybe you misjudge just how large that end table really is. Whatever the case, in the dark you cannot see everything. Most of us have learned that lesson the hard way.

When it's dark, you just don't see things as they really are. You might think you're okay, that you are fine navigating your surroundings when you really aren't fine at all. You might think you know what you are doing, but because you are in the dark, you can't really know for sure.

It's only when you turn on the light that you see everything that needs to be seen. The light reveals what might be in your way. It reveals an obstacle you could trip over. It reveals what has been left out of place. When you see it, you can adjust for it and address it.

One of the ways to know you are pure of heart is that you recognize the sin in your life and seek to address it—it is not that you don't see any sin in your life. It is when you aren't blinded to that which is creating obstacles in your path. The light lets you see the unrighteousness within you so that you can deal with it.

163

A lot of us ought to be tired by now of being spiritually blind and not being able to see the spiritual reality in front of us. We ought to be tired of stubbing our spiritual toes or banging our spiritual kneecaps or tripping over spiritual stumbling blocks. We ought to be tired of falling over things again and again rather than addressing that which is causing us to fall.

But we can only see clearly in the light. We can only see clearly when we are willing to allow the light of Christ to shine on our hearts and reveal the areas we need to address.

Spiritual sight has to do with seeing things through spiritual eyes. It has to do with recognizing the light of God and the grace He supplies. If you turn a blind eye to your own sin, you'll never even know you need God's grace. And it isn't until God's grace begins to pump through your spiritual heart that it will remove the buildup of plaque caused by sin.

One of the reasons so many of us are living such frustrated lives is because we are not able to see what God is up to. All we can see is what people are up to—what we, our mate, or our coworkers are up to. And until we discover the power of a pure heart and what it reveals spiritually, we will remain trapped by what we see physically.

Many people today try to eat organic food as much as possible. They don't want to eat the stuff that's been sprayed with pesticides. We've discovered over time that the accumulation of pesticides that we are exposed to through various foods introduces contaminants into the body that can build up over time and lead to sickness or disease. So even though you might have to pay more, or drive further to find a Whole Foods or other organic-based market, many people are willing to do that. They are willing to pay more or drive farther to get food that has not been contaminated by man.

Unfortunately, what we've allowed humanity to do is spray the pesticide of this world on our souls, and then we wonder why the heart is not working right. We wonder why our eyes aren't seeing right. We wonder why we have no spiritual zeal like the prophets of old. We wonder why we can't stay focused on God's Word for longer than a verse or two.

We have allowed the contaminants of the world to pollute our hearts so that we no longer function as God initially designed. If we will just go back to God and stop being double-minded, stop trying to find our way in the dark, stop trying to mix the world's mess with God's message, then we can discover what it means to spiritually heal. We can heal our hearts, strengthen our eyesight, and experience the well-being that comes from having all the spiritual nutrients we need to thrive.

To do that, you have to be pure in heart. You have to be willing for God to show you what is wrong or out of place so you can confess it and repent of it. Recognizing that you are poor in spirit, cultivating an awareness of your own spiritual inadequacy based on the truth of God's Word, enables you to be pure in heart. In this way, you can now see the One from whom you are to access the spiritual adequacy and fulfillment you need. Each of these kingdom virtues builds on the ones before it in some way, and they each contribute to the ones Jesus is yet to introduce as well. We will see this more clearly as we look at the final two kingdom virtues—living as a peacemaker and being persecuted for the sake of living rightly under God.

13

PEACEMAKER

In 1945, the United Nations was established. One of its primary goals was to maintain global peace. Due to the ongoing conflict and wars that had occurred over the previous decades, governing leaders sought to create a way to facilitate harmony among nations. War appeared to be so natural to the human condition, especially when it came tied to a desire for power and control. Because of this, there existed a need for an entity that would help to orchestrate peace around the world.

The United Nations established a process whereby they would seek to maintain this peace. One of the aspects of this process involved sending in peacekeeping forces to help mediate and mitigate disagreements and conflicts between nations.

Now, that might seem like a lot of effort to create an entire entity solely for the sake of keeping the peace, but historically, peace has been hard to come by. In thirty-four hundred years, there have only been two hundred sixty-eight years absent of war.* War, conflict, and jockeying for power and land have been the normal state of our world.

*Chris Hedges, "What Every Person Should Know about War," *The New York Times*, July 6, 2003, https://www.nytimes.com/2003/07/06/books/chapters/what-every-person-should-know -about-war.html.

Unfortunately, war is not only normal for nations, but it seems that it is also normal for many of us—even those of us who call ourselves Christians. It could be an internal war within an individual concerning their needs, wants, urges, and desires. Or it could show up in relational wars fought in marriage. I've seen far too many couples who look like they were joined together by the secretary of war and not a justice of the peace. Every day is a new fight or a new battle. And there are other kinds of familial conflicts, whether between parents and children or among siblings.

Some of you may feel you are entering a war zone when you go to work. It could be conflict with your supervising manager or certain coworkers. Then of course there are the cultural wars we have all experienced, especially over the last few years. Whether it concerns racial differences or political differences, social conflicts have risen in our land to a dominant place in our cultural landscape.

Whatever the case and wherever it may appear, it seems that everywhere you turn these days there is a battle. The same was true in Jesus' day as well. That's why we find that our next kingdom value has to do with keeping the peace. We read in Matthew 5:9, "Blessed are the peacemakers, for they shall be called sons of God."

To better understand what a peacemaker is, we need to look at what peace is. Peace is harmony, most notably where conflict used to exist. Peace is more than a truce. After all, two people or two nations can stop fighting physically but still live in a cold war. Some married couples assume they have peace in their relationship because they don't talk to each other. But that is not peace. That's a relational cold war. We should never be satisfied with a cold war and think that it means we have peace. Peace is much more than the removal of overt conflict. Peace includes resolving the conflict by exposing the source of the contention in order to address it.

To live with this kingdom value of peacemaking is to live as someone who does not run away from conflict, but rather faces the conflict with truth in such a way as to resolve it. A peacemaker is more than a peacekeeper. They are more than someone who stands between those in conflict and tells them not to fight. A peacemaker looks for and finds ways to resolve the conflict at hand. A peacemaker ought to be able to step back from the combatants and have them continue to get along because they have experienced a real resolution to the problem.

This is why peace must always be accompanied by righteousness. I love the way Psalm 85:10 explains this relationship: "Lovingkindness and truth have met together; righteousness and peace have kissed each other." When love and truth meet, the mouths of righteousness and peace similarly connect, producing the necessary results.

> A peacemaker looks for and finds ways to resolve the conflict at hand. A peacemaker ought to be able to step back from the combatants and have them continue to get along because they have experienced a real resolution to the problem.

Hebrews 12:14 describes the connection this way: "Pursue peace with all men, and the sanctification without which no one will see the Lord." We are to pursue peace, but we must remember that this pursuit cannot be absent of sanctification. That is, our pursuit of peace cannot succeed without the righteous requirements of God.

When Adam and Eve sinned against God, they created conflict. They created conflict with God, conflict with each other, and conflict within their own nature. This conflict resulted from their sin. It wasn't until the sin was addressed that the conflict could be addressed.

Peace is a bridge between truth and righteousness. Both truth and righteousness must exist if there is going to be any amount of lasting peace.

When a woman wants to straighten the curls in her hair, the beautician will add a chemical treatment, sometimes known as a conditioner, that will neutralize the impact of a perm. The purpose of the neutralizing agent is to keep the perm from doing chemical damage to the hair. In other words, if the perm is left in the hair and not neutralized, it will wind up doing more damage than good. Similarly, a peacemaker is someone who enters a scene of conflict in order to neutralize the conflict so that further damage is not allowed to occur.

To be a peacemaker is to be someone who is actively involved in creating harmony where conflict once existed.

REFLECTING YOUR FATHER'S CHARACTER

For those who choose to live according to this kingdom value, the blessing you will receive is that you will be "called sons of God." When a person becomes a peacemaker rather than a troublemaker, what Jesus is emphasizing is that it will be noticeable. You will be known and recognized by your fruits. Now, it doesn't change your standing with God. As a child of the King saved by faith in the sacrifice of Jesus Christ, you are a son or daughter of God. But when you live with this kingdom value as a driving emphasis in your life, you will now be "called" a son or daughter of God. People will recognize you as a kingdom disciple—a true follower of Jesus Christ.

In biblical times, to say somebody was the son of something or someone was a reflection of their character. For example, Barnabas was called the "son of consolation" because he comforted people (Acts 4:36 KJV). Judas was called the "son of perdition" (John 17:12) because of his betrayal of Jesus Christ (see Matthew 26:14–16). What people were called often revealed their reputation. This might be a personal quality as in the examples above, or it could be a parental attachment that reflects the character of the parent.

For example, you and I are children of God if we have accepted Jesus Christ as our Savior. But that doesn't mean we reflect God's character in our words and actions. To live as a peacemaker is to live as someone who truly reflects God. As a result, you will then be called, or known as, the son or daughter of God because you reflect His character.

The Bible tells us that God's character is composed of peace. We read that God is a God of peace (1 Corinthians 14:33). Jesus is known as the "Prince of Peace" (Isaiah 9:6). His birth ushers in a season of "on earth peace, good will toward men" (Luke 2:14 NKJV). Jesus told His disciples that His attribute of peace is what He would leave with them (John 14:27). In fact, when you read through the New Testament, many of the books begin with phrases like "Peace be to you."

Peace is a central component of the character of Christ. That's why to live as a peacemaker is to publicly identify with God. It is to publicly align yourself under this key kingdom virtue. When you do that, you will be blessed by being recognized as God's son or God's daughter.

To be called the son or daughter of God is to be seen as someone who knows God intimately. This is because if you share the character of God, and His character has rubbed off on your own, that means you have close contact with God. I'm sure you've seen a married couple who, over time, start to look like each other. And I'm sure you've heard a married couple finish each other's sentences. This is because, over time, they begin to rub off on each other. Their mannerisms, styles, and even expressions become more closely aligned as they spend a great amount of time together.

To be so close with God that you reflect His mannerisms, heart, and even expressions reveals this intimacy to a watching world. When you live with this kingdom value, or even with all of the kingdom values we are exploring in our time together, you are reflecting your intimacy with the King. Conversely, to live with an attitude and character of conflict, bitterness, and divisiveness reflects the closeness you share with the devil.

Satan's agenda is to create conflict. His agenda is to divide. The reason he makes this his overarching goal is because he knows that God is a God of unity, a God of peace. Any time Satan can get believers quarreling or divided, he is taking aim at the very heart of God. Satan knows that God does not inhabit division or abide in disunity.

In fact, Satan knows the Scriptures better than you and I do. He's had longer to learn them, test them, and strategize about how to supplant them. He knows 1 Peter 3:7 indicates that God won't be listening all that well to the prayers of a husband who is in conflict with his wife. It says, "You husbands in the same way, live with your wives in an understanding way, as with someone weaker, since she is a woman; and show her honor as a fellow heir of the grace of life, so that your prayers will not be hindered."

You can see why Satan is so busy seeking to create marital conflict. If he can just get a couple arguing, if he can just stir up some strife between them, he effectively strips them of their access to kingdom authority because he has removed the husband's ability to pray with the potential for impact.

That's also why Satan wants to stir things up in a family between parents and children or siblings. And why he seeks to create confusion and disorder in the church. And it is certainly why Satan works overtime on dividing people along all sorts of lines in the culture at large. The more he can divide us, the more power he has over us because he has distanced us from the only thing able to overpower him—the kingdom authority of God.

Satan is not after only you in destroying your emotions or disturbing your thoughts. In doing so, he's after everyone else as well. The more people with messed up emotions and destructive thoughts living in strife or interacting at work, the easier it is to keep people divided. And when Satan keeps people apart, he also successfully keeps them from accessing the authority of heaven in a hellish world.

When you and I resort to living as conflict-contributors rather than as peacemakers, we have inadvertently chosen sides. We have aligned ourselves with the agenda of the devil. God is a God of harmony and oneness. That doesn't mean we all have to agree or see things the same way, but it does mean that in our disagreements, we express ourselves in a way that demonstrates we are unified on a common goal—that of advancing God's kingdom agenda on earth.

If we can agree on that, we might be surprised at how many other things we can agree on. Unity is a powerful thing. We read in Matthew 18:19–20,

> "Again I say to you, that if two of you agree on earth about anything that they may ask, it shall be done for them by My Father who is in heaven. For where two or three have gathered together in My name, I am there in their midst."

Jesus comes down and takes His place as the centerpiece among us where agreement and unity exist. Keep in mind that when Jesus shows up, His power and His authority show up too.

Thus, you can see why it is in the devil's interest to break up the agreements between people. It is in the devil's interest to cause division and stoke the embers of envy, disunity, and distrust. When he does that, we fall into the trap of limiting our own prayers to God.

Far too many of us are actually blocking the movement of God in our lives because we are living in ongoing conflict. Or we are blocking the authority of God to overpower the enemy and his tactics in our lives because we are engaged in disunity.

When our emotions and our thoughts are war zones because we refuse to be unified under God and His kingdom authority, we pay the price. You might think that when you are angry at someone or when you are judging someone you disagree with that you are harming or dismissing them. But you are actually harming and dismissing yourself. The more conflict you carry in your own heart, the more chaos you invite into your life and circumstances.

Blessed are the peacemakers because they will carry the powerful testimony of the power of God. To be blessed is to have God show up when you need Him most. It is to see God's hand in the midst of your trials and challenges. It is to experience the authority of God as He overturns, overrides, or removes that which Satan has sent to take you down. A blessing isn't a pat on your head or an "attaboy." A blessing accesses power, opportunities, and kingdom authority. A blessing opens doors.

Many of you may be familiar with the story of the man sitting outside of the White House in the mid-1800s. He had taken a seat on one of the available park benches. Shortly after sitting down, he began to cry. A little boy came up to him and asked him what was wrong. The man told the little boy that he had a big family issue that only the president could solve. But as he said those words, his voice shook because he continued, "But they won't let me go in to see the president."

That's when the little boy took him by the hand and asked him to come with him. They walked past the guards. They walked past the barriers. They walked past the inner guards. And then they walked into the Oval Office, where the boy said, "Dad, this man wants to talk to you." President Lincoln then turned to the man and gave him his attention. In other words, because of the son's relationship to the father, President Lincoln, and because of the man's relationship to the son, doors were opened for him that he would not have been able to walk through on his own.

Living according to the kingdom value of being a peacemaker isn't just for monks or nuns or people marching for peace. This is a critical kingdom value that, if you will adopt it as a way of life, will open the floodgates of heaven for you. This divine recognition of your sonship or daughtership of God gives you instant access to the King. It gives you access to answered prayer. You get to hear from heaven, whereas before your prayers often bounced off the ceiling. You will be blessed.

PEACE THROUGH THE CROSS

You access your blessing as you engage the Holy Spirit's work in your life so that you can enjoy the peace Jesus came to give. The way you get this peace is by the blood of Christ. Jesus provides you with peace through the cross. Let's look at this more closely in Ephesians 2:13–18, which says,

> But now in Christ Jesus you who formerly were far off have been brought near by the blood of Christ. For He Himself is our peace, who made both groups into one and broke down the barrier of the dividing wall, by abolishing in His flesh the enmity, which is the Law of commandments contained in ordinances, so that in Himself He might make the two into one new man, thus establishing peace, and might reconcile them both in one body to God through the cross, by it having put to death the enmity. AND HE CAME AND PREACHED PEACE TO YOU WHO WERE FAR AWAY, AND PEACE TO THOSE WHO WERE NEAR; for through Him we both have our access in one Spirit to the Father.

An important point to remember is that the cross is a painful place. It is a place of blood, judgment, nails, and spears. It's not a pretty place or a cute event, as we sometimes try to make it by decorating our homes with crosses. Grief takes place at the cross because it is the location where sin is atoned for.

The cross is ugly and painful because that is where Jesus shed His blood so He could offer you and me the peace we desperately long for and need. The only reason we can be blessed and experience peace is because Jesus took our punishment on the cross. The blood that covers our personal sin to provide us with access to personal peace is the same blood that covers the sins of others. If you want to be a peacemaker in other people's lives or even within your own relationships, you have to apply the blood so it will address and cover the sin. It is the blood of Christ that brings about the peace. And the way we apply the blood is by addressing the sin and repenting of it. If we fail to deal with the sin that is causing the conflict, we will also fail to live as peacemakers.

It is always the role of a peacemaker to help others identify the sin that is causing the chaos so it can be addressed. Most of the conflict in our world is allowed to remain and take root because no one wants to deal with the sin that started it. But the Bible tells us, "'There is no peace for the wicked,' says the LORD" (Isaiah 48:22). When individuals or entities refuse to address the sin in a way that honors God, they can forget about experiencing peace.

You can spend the rest of your life as a Christian in perpetual conflict if you are unwilling to recognize, address, and remove the sin in your life. We must rip up the root if we are ever going to remove the rotten fruit sin has caused all around us, and even within us. We do this by returning to the truth. Truth reveals sin because truth is based on an absolute standard by which righteousness is measured.

> **Most of the conflict in our world is allowed to remain and take root because no one wants to deal with the sin that started it.**

When I get my bank statement and it comes time for me to balance my checkbook or my own personal record of spending and the two don't agree, I can't just shrug it off. I can't just say that I prefer the amount I have recorded over the bank's amount. If my personal spending log and the bank statement disagree, I'm going to need to reconcile it. The only way to reconcile a bank statement with your personal account of spending is to locate where the problem lies. Once you can identify the problem, you can correct the problem. You don't skip locating the error if you really want to know what you have available.

Similarly, you can't skip sin and just say everything is going to be all right. If you and God are not on the same page regarding the errors and issues in your life, or in the lives of those around you whom He's asking you to help discover peace, you will not gain access to real peace. You might pretend you have peace just like I could pretend I have more money in my account. But it is only in the reconciliation that you will discover what you truly have and be able to use it.

Swedish physicist Alfred Bernhard Nobel created dynamite. His intentions were pure in that he wanted to create an explosive that could be used to move rock so roads could be built or buildings be erected. He wanted to create a force powerful enough to open up channels for transportation. He wanted to make life better.

The problem is that people took Nobel's invention and used it in a way he never intended. They used his dynamite for destruction and even brought about large-scale death. Seeing what became of his invention, Nobel set out to counteract it. He set out to incentivize people who would counteract the destruction. He took his own funds and began to award people who promoted peace. Over time, the people who were honored became known as Nobel Peace Prize winners.

The people who received this award were those who sought to make peace, not war. They sought to live as peacemakers, not troublemakers.

God is looking for His own award winners. He is looking for some Jesus Peace Prize winners to bless. He wants to see who is using His gifts and His creation for good and not for evil. He wants to see who is applying the blood of Jesus Christ to situations and conflicts in life to usher in peace. God wants to bless you. But He's asking you to do something to show that you are positioned for this blessing of His. He's asking you to step up and step into the midst of the chaos and confusion both within and without and seek to bring about peace.

14

PERSECUTED FOR RIGHTEOUSNESS

I commend you for opening up this last chapter. Many people reading this book might not do so. It takes courage to read about this remaining kingdom value because this one comes with some sacrifice. Jesus has just gone through a variety of kingdom values we should live by if we want to experience a blessed life, but the one He ends on might make most of us nervous. Jesus didn't mince His words, so neither should I. Let's get right to it. The final kingdom value we are to embrace and live out is told to us like this: "Blessed are those who have been persecuted for the sake of righteousness, for theirs is the kingdom of heaven" (Matthew 5:10).

Now, if that didn't scare you enough to close this book, Jesus takes a moment to emphasize this one. Each of the other kingdom values is delivered in one succinct sentence. But this one gets a double punch. Jesus continues, just in case anyone missed what He said,

"Blessed are you when people insult you and persecute you, and falsely say all kinds of evil against you because of Me. Rejoice and be glad, for your reward in heaven is great; for in the same way they persecuted the prophets who were before you."

vv. 11–12

Notice that this double-punch kingdom value also comes with a double blessing. Every other value gives you one blessing, but this one doubles the fun. This blessing refers not only to what you can receive while on earth through the presence of Jesus Christ and His favor in your life, but also to the "treasures" you lay up in heaven (see Matthew 6:19–20). Jesus reminds His listeners that you are doubly blessed when you are persecuted, insulted, and maligned for the sake of righteousness and His kingdom.

But even though He says it clearly and says it twice, it still seems to be incongruent because we don't normally associate a blessing with hardship and persecution. When we dig deeper into the meaning of the Greek term translated as "persecuted," it makes it even more difficult to see the connection. The literal translation means to be harassed. It refers to being treated in an evil, negative manner. This can include insults, abuse, vicious speech, and even false accusations.

Just writing those things down makes me wince. It probably does the same to you when you read them. None of us enjoys being bullied or volunteers for harassment. But Jesus concludes His emphasis on kingdom values by saying we are blessed for being bullied for righteousness' sake. Keep in mind, He doesn't say you and I are blessed for being bullied for any other reason. The blessing is tied to the "why."

This blessing is given to those who are persecuted or harassed for the sake of His name, His righteousness, or His kingdom agenda. This type of persecution comes about when you are choosing to do the right thing or say the right thing for righteous reasons and you face fallout for your choice. When you face persecution tied to the fact that you are living out the values of the kingdom of God and you are associated with Jesus Christ, that is when you can expect a blessing.

Keep in mind, the blessing is a bonus. Because Scripture often tells us that when you follow Christ as King, you will face adversity. There will be opposition. Paul says, "Indeed, all who desire to live godly in Christ Jesus will be persecuted" (2 Timothy 3:12). If and when you choose to live as a kingdom disciple, you are checking the box in the terms that says "Willing to be persecuted." That's just part of the deal.

In fact, if you are not facing spiritual persecution or opposition of any kind, then you can assume that you are not living a godly life based on kingdom values. If there are absolutely no negative repercussions coming your way because of your faith and the choices you make based on it, then your faith is not being clearly demonstrated. You are a secret-agent Christian, or a spiritual CIA operative. Persecution is part and parcel of the process of kingdom living.

When you decided to live as a visible Christian because you wanted to align yourself with the value system of the kingdom of God, you chose to be a problem in this postmodern age, when Christian values are no longer the normative value system of the culture. The further a culture moves away from a Christian world view, the more those who live according to kingdom values will appear to be peculiar and will be persecuted.

Now, to appear peculiar doesn't mean you are to be intentionally weird. It just means you will stand out as stepping to the beat of a different drummer. You will set yourself apart from the crowd as

> If there are absolutely no negative repercussions coming your way because of your faith and the choices you make based on it, then your faith is not being clearly demonstrated. You are a secret-agent Christian. Persecution is part and parcel of the process of kingdom living.

someone who listens to a different voice and adheres to a different standard called righteousness. Jesus' standard of kingdom values is diametrically opposed to the world's values. When you choose to embrace His kingdom standard as a lifestyle, you will invite spiritual persecution or harassment into your world.

I am sure that you had someone in your class in school, as I did, who would "set the curve." When the teacher said he or she would grade on a curve, that meant the highest score would serve as the perfect score. In that case, most of us hoped that the highest score wouldn't be all that high. But there was always somebody who would ace it, it seems. There was always someone who had to ruin the blessing of the curve for the rest of us.

See, the problem with Jesus is that whenever He, or His kingdom values, shows up—He messes with the world's curve. He sets the standard too high. He raises the bar. As long as people can compare themselves with other people, everyone passes. But when Jesus and His kingdom values appear, problems pop up for everyone else. Jesus reveals the righteous standards of God.

And when you and I choose to live according to these righteous standards, we make other people—and their lower standards—look bad. We demonstrate that peace is more productive than chaos. We demonstrate that love is more powerful than hate. We reveal that families can stay together and employees can work hard, even when no one is around to see what they are doing. We raise the standard, and in doing so, we invite persecution.

Nobody likes someone else to show up and reveal just how far behind they are lagging. Jesus did that when He came to earth. And we do that as His kingdom disciples when we live out the kingdom values He's established for us. So, just as Jesus was persecuted when He walked down here, we can expect the same. In fact, He tells us that in John 15:20–21. We read,

> "Remember the word that I said to you, 'A slave is not greater than
> his master.' If they persecuted Me, they will also persecute you; if

they kept My word, they will keep yours also. But all these things they will do to you for My name's sake, because they do not know the One who sent Me."

In other words, what they did to Jesus they will do to you when you choose to follow Jesus as your Lord and King. As you adopt more and more kingdom values, you will be manifesting the presence of Christ to others. The same level of hate, vitriol, and persecution that He experienced has the potential to come at you as well.

VALUE SYSTEM CONFLICT

The reason so many of us do not face any spiritual persecution is because we are not living with kingdom values. When the world looks at our value system, it doesn't see much that is different from its own. We give in because we want to be accepted. We don't stand up for righteousness because we don't want to be labeled weird. We try to get by, attending church only every once in a while because we don't want to come across as a fully committed follower of Christ. But in doing so, we also miss out on the blessing. The blessing comes to those who are persecuted for the sake of righteousness. It doesn't just come to those who call themselves Christians.

You are blessed when you operate by the divine standard called righteousness. You are blessed when you publicly associate with Jesus Christ through your choices and behavior.

In the past, we often saw great hatred toward our nation in the Middle East, and one of the primary reasons was our association with Israel. Since Israel was hated deeply by many nations in the Middle East, our public association with Israel brought hatred to us as well. What Jesus is saying in this final kingdom value is that when you publicly align with Him and claim His kingdom value system as your own, others are going to feel about you what they feel about Him. And since they obviously didn't want Him—they crucified Him even—you can expect the same level of disdain toward you.

The issue you'll face when you adopt a kingdom value system is that it conflicts with the system of this world order. There's a clash of opinions that will show up in how you are treated. Adopting the values of the kingdom will create issues and provoke insults. It could negatively impact your potential for promotion at work, as well as affect who likes you on the job. When you live and speak according to the ethics of the kingdom, it will affect your associations elsewhere. This is because living with a kingdom value system in a world that doesn't buy into it will invite rejection and hate.

Last I checked, none of us wants to experience rejection or hate. And it's natural not to want these things in your life. So in order to truly live according to the kingdom value system, you're going to need to resist the urge to tweak it to fit the culture. You're going to need to resist your internal impulse to stay under the radar of those around you. You're going to need to dig deep and discover the courage required to stand up in defense of the truth, which is so frequently attacked and maligned today.

You can't change the kingdom values and still access the blessing. You can't rewrite them and expect to get the favor from God that is tied to them. His blessing comes when you adopt His values and live them out in your life.

What God desires in establishing this incentivized kingdom value system is maintaining a standard of righteousness in an evil-infiltrated world. He has not changed His standard just because society ignores it. He desires that we rise up to it as a way of manifesting Him and His presence to those around us. When we do that, we call attention to Him. We bring Him glory. We honor Him as we point out just how far off the mark Satan's world order truly is, as well as those who have chosen to operate by it.

When you and I carry the light of kingdom values within our spheres of influence, we reflect God's standard to others. We help them to see where they need to adjust, repent, and grow. Sure, they might not like that or appreciate it. But if they respond to God's kingdom standard, they will eventually be blessed too.

I know you still might be scratching your head as you read through this last chapter. Because so far, we've only focused on the bad. And if the negatives associated with the kingdom value system exist on such a high level, then it is confusing how it can be called a blessing. But that's exactly what Jesus calls it—twice.

In fact, Jesus emphasizes how much of a blessing it is when He tells us to "rejoice and be glad" about any persecution we face for righteousness' sake. And the reason we can rejoice with praise is because of what we get in return. Jesus says we ought to be able to smile when we are persecuted because we are assured that ours "is the kingdom of heaven."

We saw this phrase earlier when we studied what it means to be poor in spirit. It's a bookend phrase that surrounds the kingdom values we are to live out. What it means is that the people who experience negative repercussions due to their identification with Christ and His kingdom values will also get to see heaven overrule earth. Instead of being entwined and trapped in the kingdom of earth, where men or the devil and his minions rule, you will get to see the kingdom of heaven, where God rules.

When it appears that the earth's kingdom is keeping you from moving ahead either by denying you a promotion or excluding you from activities, you will get to see what happens when God demonstrates that He is the ultimate ruler and potentate over all. Society might seek to control your mind, your emotions, and even your productivity—but society will have to yield to God when you invite Him to intervene. If you hold to His kingdom value system, He will override the systems of this age.

As a kingdom follower, you will know what it means for the supernatural to invade the natural. You will know firsthand what it looks like for heaven to invade history. You'll get to experience eternity overruling earth. You'll get to see what God looks like when He shows up and shows out on your behalf.

One of the reasons so many of us have never seen God overrule anything or anyone in our lives is because we've not chosen to live according to kingdom values. We've never had a situation where God saw that we were acting and speaking according to His kingdom values so that He could act and speak in defense of us. God doesn't intervene just because we need it. He intervenes when He sees that we have chosen to live according to His standard.

> As a kingdom follower, you will know what it means for the supernatural to invade the natural, for heaven to invade history. You'll get to see what God looks like when He shows up and shows out on your behalf.

If you choose not to identify with the person or values of the King, you don't get to see the kingdom of heaven overruling the kingdom of men.

One of my most graphic experiences of this happened when I was working at a transit station unloading vehicles overnight while attending seminary. Shortly after I started working there, I was introduced to a scheme. The scheme involved punching each other out and back in on the time cards so that people could go sleep for a few hours during the shift. It was set up on a rotation basis so that everyone got a nap at some point in the week.

But when they explained the scheme to me, I told them I couldn't participate in it. I explained that it would be considered stealing to sleep on the job like that. They proceeded to pressure me and tell me that everyone was doing it, but I didn't back down. As you might imagine, that earned me the nickname of "Rev," as well as a few other names I won't put in this book. What's more, it also earned me the opportunity to load and unload vehicles without any help. They decided they would teach me a lesson for not taking part in their scheme. To be honest, it was rough. Month after month I was often left to load and unload the heavy bags alone because I wouldn't play their game.

After about three months of this, I got a call from the manager's office. The manager wanted me to come and talk to him after I got off work at seven in the morning. As I made my way to the office, I couldn't imagine what he wanted to talk to me about. But what he said surprised me. And it perfectly illustrated what Jesus had said in His Sermon on the Mount. I had studied the sermon in seminary, but God gave me a bird's-eye view of it in person.

When I got to the office, the manager explained that they had sent a supervisor undercover to have a look at how the night shift was performing. In the midst of checking out the employees and their work ethic, they discovered the scheme. He explained that they were fully aware of employees' clocking each other in or out so that someone could go get some sleep. He said they were also fully aware that I did not participate in the scheme. As a result, he said, smiling, they wanted to promote me to be the night supervisor so that I could oversee everyone else. Not only that, but they also gave me a raise.

This is just one of many such examples God has allowed me to experience, but they never get old. Getting to see heaven overrule earth when you play by God's rules and keep His kingdom values first and foremost in your life is one of life's greatest blessings. Sure, the blessing is preceded by insults and possibly even rejection. But when you get to see God show up in a way you never could have imagined—a way you had only heard about on Sunday morning but never experienced for yourself—that's when God becomes real. That's when He starts to take shape in your life in such a way that you can say you truly know Him.

We are to rejoice and be glad in the face of spiritually based harassment, similar to how the saints in the book of Acts said they rejoiced in the midst of suffering for their identification with Jesus Christ. The reason we rejoice is because it ultimately means that heaven is on our side.

Far too many of us live miserable lives because earth is on our side, not heaven. Eternity and the authority tied to it are not obligated to enter history and act on our behalf if we refuse to live with kingdom values. God gets involved when He sees that you and I are honoring His goal of advancing His kingdom agenda on earth.

A lot of people want to presume that they are blessed and highly favored. They want to speak as if they have the Lord fighting their battles for them. But breathing is not a guarantee of God's divine intervention. Being alive on earth does not bind Him to your side. The way you get God's rule to overrule the chaos of the culture and the confusion in your circumstances is by aligning yourself under His rule. You do that by living out the kingdom values based on His truth that we have looked at in this book.

It starts with recognizing your own spiritual inadequacy. You begin by being poor in spirit. Then you add to that a willingness to be honest about your sin and to mourn its existence in your life or in our land. Doing so enables you to then apply the kingdom value of gentleness to your words and your actions.

In addition to gentleness, and as you begin to see God's blessings begin to flow more and more into your life, you develop a greater hunger and thirst for His righteousness. You pursue Him and His truth at a higher level because you want to apply His thoughts, His perspective, and His rule to your life. As you do, you'll discover that you have a greater ability to show mercy to others. You will also start to live with a purity of heart that allows you to see God and His ways more clearly than before. This will inspire you to be a peacemaker rather than a troublemaker in all you do and say.

And, as you will discover, living according to those kingdom values will bring upon you a level of persecution—insult, rejection, harassment—you've never known before. But you will see, as I did at the transit station, that even though your back might be tired from loading and unloading the baggage all by yourself, God will have your back. He will show up when you least expect it. And He will turn things around in your favor.

Remember also that this kingdom value comes with a second blessing. As we saw earlier, the reason you can rejoice and be glad in the face of persecution is because your "reward in heaven is great." You will get an eternal reward.

ETERNAL BLESSINGS

In the last days before my wife, Lois, went on to glory, she lived in a state of in-between. The effects of the cancer had taken away much of her physical strength, so she slept a lot and even saw things that we couldn't see. For example, one time she asked us if we could see her mom and dad, both of whom had died previously, sitting in the room with us. Of course we couldn't, but we know she did.

In one of these in-between moments, Lois expressed delight. She said, "The award, the award." We asked her what award she was talking about. She said they were wanting to give her an award and that they were just waiting for the music to start. We were blessed to gain a glimpse into what she saw so clearly and would get to experience so fully in eternity. There is no way to explain to any of us who are still on earth what an eternal award will be like, but I do know it will be worth whatever you have to face in achieving it.

Friend, as you make your life choices in the ordinary moments of each day, know that each one matters. Each decision you make, every word you say is being watched by your loving heavenly Father. He desires to reward you for following Him. He has an abundance of treasures and awards stored up to give to those who choose to live as kingdom disciples. As you begin to apply His kingdom values to your life, you will be opening the door to experiencing these blessings ever more so on earth and later in eternity. You'll also be influencing those around you with the light of God's love as you spread the truth of His Word to a world in need.

KINDNESS CHALLENGE

The atmosphere in our contemporary culture has become contaminated and saturated with hatred, racism, crime, meanness, disrespect, and a myriad of other expressions of insensitivity and vitriol. We are in desperate need of a movement of kindness that can spread like wildfire across the land to reclaim the civility necessary for us to have a peaceful, friendly environment in which to live, work, raise our kids, and bring stability in a nation of decline.

Therefore, our national ministry, the Urban Alternative, has launched a national campaign called Kindness in the Culture. It is a simple Christian initiative that can be implemented by individuals, families, churches, civic organizations, and the like.

You simply take an act of kindness card and seek to do some deed of kindness each week for a friend, neighbor, coworker, or stranger who has a need. This can include buying a meal for a homeless person, helping an elderly person across the street, babysitting for a couple so they can have a night out, comforting a distraught neighbor, or countless other ways to help out another person who is hurting.

The key to this initiative is that the act of kindness is to be accompanied by praying with the person you assist regarding their immediate need as well as their ongoing well-being, spiritual development, and any other request they might have. You then also seek to share the good news of the gospel with them if applicable. This makes your act of kindness not just a "good thing" but what the Bible calls a "good work," since God is directly attached to the act.

Acts of kindness cards can be ordered from our ministry website (tonyevans.org) and then customized for you, your church, or your group if you so desire so that those you help can become connected to greater spiritual and social impact. Or you can simply design and print your own. The idea behind the cards is to give the person something to point them to God so they know the motivation behind this act of kindness. The cards can also be used to invite them to your particular church or to leave them with a Scripture verse.

This plan is simple, replicable, and easily transferable. If we can get millions of Christians to lead the way in doing this at least once a week, we can greatly contribute to changing the atmosphere of our culture for good and for God.

It's time for believers to let people see our good works and not just hear our good words so that they glorify our Father in heaven (Matthew 5:13–16). The world needs a new value system through the Kindness in the Culture initiative so that we can advance a kingdom values paradigm for the improvement of lives and the greater glory of God.

Dr. Tony Evans, Dallas, Texas

ACKNOWLEDGMENTS

I want to thank my friends at Baker Publishing Group for their interest and partnership in bringing my thoughts, study, and words to print on this valuable subject. I particularly want to thank Andy McGuire for leading the charge on this manuscript with Baker Publishing Group. It's been a pleasure working with Andy to see this through to print. I also want to publicly thank Sharon Hodge and Hannah Ahlfield. In addition, my appreciation goes out to Heather Hair for her skills and insights in writing and collaborating on this manuscript.

APPENDIX

THE URBAN ALTERNATIVE

The Urban Alternative (TUA) equips, empowers, and unites Christians to impact *individuals*, *families*, *churches*, and *communities* through a thoroughly kingdom agenda and world view. In teaching truth, we seek to transform lives.

The core cause of the problems we face in our personal lives, homes, churches, and societies is a spiritual one; therefore, the only way to address it is spiritually. We've tried a political, social, economic, and even a religious agenda.

It's time for a **kingdom agenda**.

> *The kingdom agenda can be defined as the visible manifestation of the comprehensive rule of God over every area of life.*

The unifying central theme throughout the Bible is the glory of God and the advancement of His kingdom. The conjoining thread from Genesis to Revelation—from beginning to end—is focused on one thing: God's glory through advancing God's kingdom.

When you do not recognize that theme, the Bible becomes disconnected stories that are great for inspiration but seem to be unrelated in purpose and direction. Understanding the role of the kingdom in Scripture increases the relevance of this several-thousand-year-old text to your day-to-day living, because the kingdom is not only then; it is now.

The absence of the kingdom's influence in our personal lives, family lives, churches, and communities has led to a deterioration in our world of immense proportions:

- People live segmented, compartmentalized lives because they lack God's kingdom world view.
- Families disintegrate because they exist for their own satisfaction rather than for the kingdom.
- Churches are limited in the scope of their impact because they fail to comprehend that the goal of the church is not the church itself, but the kingdom.
- Communities have nowhere to turn to find real solutions for real people who have real problems because the church has become divided, ingrown, and unable to transform the cultural and political landscape in any relevant way.

The kingdom agenda offers us a way to see and live life with a solid hope by optimizing the solutions of heaven. When God is no longer the final and authoritative standard under which all else falls, order and hope leave with Him. But the reverse of that is true as well: as long as you have God, you have hope. If God is still in the picture, and as long as His agenda is still on the table, it's not over.

Even if relationships collapse, God will sustain you. Even if finances dwindle, God will keep you. Even if dreams die, God will revive you. As long as God and His rule are still the overarching standard in your life, family, church, and community, there is always hope.

Our world needs the King's agenda. Our churches need the King's agenda. Our families need the King's agenda.

We've put together a three-part plan to direct us in healing the divisions and striving for unity as we move toward the goal of truly being one nation under God. This three-part plan calls us to assemble with others in unity, address the issues that divide us, and act together for social impact. Following this plan, we will see individuals, families, churches, and communities transformed as we follow God's kingdom agenda in every area of our lives. You can request this plan by emailing info@tonyevans.org, or you can find it online at tonyevans.org.

In many major cities, there is a loop that drivers can take when they want to get somewhere on the other side of the city but don't necessarily want to head straight through downtown. This loop will take you close enough to the city so that you can see its towering buildings and skyline, but not close enough to actually experience it.

This is precisely what we, as a culture, have done with God. We have put Him on the "loop" of our personal, family, church, and community lives. He's close enough to be at hand should we need Him in an emergency, but far enough away that He can't be the center of who we are.

We want God on the loop, not the King of the Bible who comes downtown into the very heart of our ways. Leaving God on the loop brings about dire consequences, as we have seen in our own lives and with others. But when we make God, and His rule, the centerpiece of all we think, do, and say, it is then that we will experience Him in the way He longs for us to experience Him.

He wants us to be kingdom people with kingdom minds set on fulfilling His kingdom's purposes. He wants us to pray, as Jesus did, "Not my will, but Thy will be done." Because His is the kingdom, the power, and the glory.

There is only one God, and we are not Him. As King and Creator, God calls the shots. It is only when we align ourselves underneath His comprehensive hand that we will access His full power and authority in all spheres of life: personal, familial, ecclesiastical, and governmental.

As we learn how to govern ourselves under God, we then transform the institutions of family, church, and society using a biblically based kingdom world view.

Under Him, we touch heaven and change earth.

To achieve our goal, we use a variety of strategies, approaches, and resources for reaching and equipping as many people as possible.

BROADCAST MEDIA

Millions of individuals experience *The Alternative with Dr. Tony Evans* through the daily radio broadcast playing on nearly **1,400 radio outlets** and in over **130 countries**. The broadcast can also be seen on several television networks and is available online at tonyevans.org. You can also listen to or view the daily broadcast by downloading the Tony Evans app for free in the App store. Over 30 million message downloads or streams occur each year.

LEADERSHIP TRAINING

The Tony Evans Training Center (TETC) facilitates a comprehensive discipleship platform that embodies Dr. Tony Evans's ministry philosophy as expressed through the kingdom agenda. The training courses focus on leadership development and discipleship in these five tracks:

- ▸ Bible and theology
- ▸ Personal growth
- ▸ Family and relationships
- ▸ Church health and leadership development
- ▸ Society and community impact strategies

The TETC program includes courses for both local and online students. Furthermore, TETC programming includes course work for non-student attendees. Pastors, Christian leaders and Christian laity, both local and at a distance, can seek out the Kingdom Agenda Certificate for personal, spiritual, and professional development. For more information, visit tonyevanstraining.org.

Kingdom Agenda Pastors (KAP) provides a viable network for *like-minded pastors* who embrace the kingdom agenda philosophy. Pastors have the opportunity to go deeper with Dr. Tony Evans as they are given greater biblical knowledge, practical applications, and resources to impact individuals, families, churches, and communities. KAP welcomes *senior and associate pastors* of all churches. KAP also offers an annual summit held each year in Dallas with intensive seminars, workshops, and resources. For more information, visit kafellowship.org.

Pastors' Wives Ministry, founded by Dr. Lois Evans, provides *counsel, encouragement*, and *spiritual resources* for pastors' wives as they serve with their husbands in the ministry. A primary focus of the ministry is the KAP Summit that offers senior pastors' wives a safe place to *reflect, renew*, and *relax* along with training in personal development, spiritual growth, and care for their emotional and physical well-being. For more information, visit loisevans.org.

KINGDOM COMMUNITY IMPACT

The outreach programs of the Urban Alternative seek to positively impact individuals, churches, families, and communities through a variety of ministries. We see these efforts as necessary to our calling as a ministry and essential to the communities we serve. With training on how to initiate and maintain programs to adopt schools, or provide homeless services, or partner toward unity and justice with the local police precincts, which creates a connection between the police and our community, we, as a ministry, live out

God's kingdom agenda according to our Kingdom Strategy for Community Transformation.

The Kingdom Strategy for Community Transformation is a three-part plan that equips churches to have a positive impact on their communities for the kingdom of God. It also provides numerous practical suggestions for how this three-part plan can be implemented in your community, and it serves as a blueprint for unifying churches around the common goal of creating a better world for all of us. For more information, visit tonyevans.org and click on the link to access the 3-Point Plan.

National Church Adopt-a-School Initiative (NCAASI) prepares churches across the country to impact communities by using *public schools as the primary vehicle for effecting positive social change* in urban youth and families. Leaders of churches, school districts, faith-based organizations, and other nonprofit organizations are equipped with the knowledge and tools to *forge partnerships* and build *strong social service delivery systems*. This training is based on the comprehensive church-based community impact strategy conducted by Oak Cliff Bible Fellowship. It addresses such areas as economic development, education, housing, health revitalization, family renewal, and racial reconciliation. We assist churches in tailoring the model to meet specific needs of their communities while simultaneously addressing the spiritual and moral frame of reference. Training events are held annually in the Dallas area at Oak Cliff Bible Fellowship. For more information, visit churchadoptaschool.org.

Athlete's Impact (AI) exists as an outreach both into and through the sports arena. Coaches can be the most influential individuals in young people's lives, even ahead of their parents. With the growing rise of fatherlessness in our culture, more young people are looking to their coaches for guidance, character development, practical needs, and hope. After coaches on the influencer scale fall athletes. Athletes (whether professional or amateur) influence younger athletes and kids within their spheres of impact. Knowing this, we have made it our aim to equip and train coaches and athletes on how to live out and utilize their God-given roles for the benefit of the kingdom. We aim to do this through our iCoach App as well as resources such as *The Playbook: A Life Strategy Guide for Athletes*. For more information, visit icoachapp.org.

Tony Evans Films ushers in positive life change through compelling video shorts, animation, and feature-length films. We seek to build kingdom disciples through the power of story. We use a variety of platforms for viewer consumption and have over 100 million digital views. We also merge video shorts and film with relevant Bible study materials to bring people to the saving knowledge of Jesus Christ and to strengthen the body of Christ worldwide. Tony Evans Films released its first feature-length film, *Kingdom Men Rising*, in April 2019 in over 800 theaters nationwide, in partnership with LifeWay Films. The second release, *Journey With Jesus*, in partnership with RightNow Media, was released in theaters in November 2021.

RESOURCE DEVELOPMENT

We are fostering lifelong learning partnerships with the people we serve by providing a variety of published materials. Dr. Evans has published more than 125 unique titles based on over 50 years of preaching, including booklets, books, and Bible studies. He also holds the honor of writing and publishing the first full-Bible commentary and study Bible by an African American, which released in 2019. This Bible sits in permanent display as a historic release in the Museum of the Bible in Washington, DC.

For more information, and a complimentary copy of Dr. Evans's devotional newsletter, call (800) 800-3222, write TUA at P.O. Box 4000, Dallas, TX 75208, or visit tonyevans.org

ABOUT THE AUTHOR

Dr. Tony Evans is one of the country's most respected leaders in evangelical circles. He is a pastor, bestselling author, and frequent speaker at Bible conferences and seminars throughout the nation.

Dr. Evans has served as the senior pastor of Oak Cliff Bible Fellowship for over forty years, witnessing it grow from ten people in 1976 to now over 10,000 congregants and over 100 ministries.

He also serves as president of the Urban Alternative, a national ministry that seeks to restore hope and transform lives through the proclamation and application of the Word of God. His daily radio broadcast, *The Alternative with Dr. Tony Evans*, can be heard on over 1,400 radio outlets throughout the United States and in more than 130 countries.

Dr. Evans holds the honor of writing and publishing the first full-Bible commentary and study Bible by an African American. The study Bible and commentary went on to sell more than 225,000 copies in the first year.

He is the former chaplain for the Dallas Cowboys and the Dallas Mavericks.

Through his local church and national ministry, Dr. Evans has set in motion a kingdom-agenda philosophy of ministry that teaches

God's comprehensive rule over every area of life as demonstrated through the individual, the family, the church, and society.

Dr. Evans was married to Lois, his wife and ministry partner of over 50 years, until Lois transitioned to glory in late 2019. They are the proud parents of four, grandparents of thirteen, and great-grandparents of three.

More from Tony Evans

In his thought-provoking book, Dr. Tony Evans challenges you to foster personal discipleship and lead others, taking the next step to become the powerful man of God you were made to be. Evans brings his insights, stories, and wise counsel from God's Word to help you stop settling for a faith that goes through the motions and leave a legacy of faith.

Kingdom Men Rising

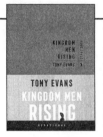

When it comes to becoming all God created you to be, the daily reminders in this 90-day devotional from Dr. Tony Evans will help you walk in victory and faith to make an impact on others for God. They will also challenge you to foster personal discipleship and apply a leadership mindset so that you can be led to the abundant life you've been called to.

Kingdom Men Rising Devotional

BETHANYHOUSE

Stay up to date on your favorite books and authors with our free e-newsletters. Sign up today at bethanyhouse.com.

 facebook.com/BHPnonfiction

 @bethany_house

 @bethany_house_nonfiction